# Am I My Sister's Keeper?

## Bible Studies for Women

### Barbara Geer

WestBow
PRESS

Copyright © 2012 by Barbara Geer.

All rights reserved. No part of this book may be used or reproduced by any means, graphic, electronic, or mechanical, including photocopying, recording, taping or by any information storage retrieval system without the written permission of the publisher except in the case of brief quotations embodied in critical articles and reviews.

WestBow Press books may be ordered through booksellers or by contacting:

WestBow Press
A Division of Thomas Nelson
1663 Liberty Drive
Bloomington, IN 47403
www.westbowpress.com
1-(866) 928-1240

Because of the dynamic nature of the Internet, any web addresses or links contained in this book may have changed since publication and may no longer be valid. The views expressed in this work are solely those of the author and do not necessarily reflect the views of the publisher, and the publisher hereby disclaims any responsibility for them.

Any people depicted in stock imagery provided by Thinkstock are models, and such images are being used for illustrative purposes only.

Certain stock imagery © Thinkstock.

ISBN: 978-1-4497-6900-0 (sc)

Library of Congress Control Number: 2012918119

Printed in the United States of America

WestBow Press rev. date: 10/02/2012

# TABLE OF CONTENTS

1. AND THEN SOME ................................................................. 1
2. ORGANIZATION—HOW IS THIS A SPIRITUAL MATTER? ....... 7
3. AM I MY SISTER'S KEEPER? ............................................... 13
4. GROWING IN FAITH TOGETHER Part 1 ............................. 19
5. GROWING IN FAITH TOGETHER Part 2 ............................. 23
6. WITH ALL MY HEART ........................................................ 27
7. ABOVE ALL ....................................................................... 31
8. WORDS OF LIFE ................................................................ 37
9. SHHH! LISTEN . . . ............................................................. 41
10. ESTHER—WOMAN OF COURAGE ..................................... 45
11. I AM GOD'S WORKMANSHIP ............................................ 51
12. GOD'S WORD—DIGGING DEEPER .................................... 55
13. DID YOU DO THIS FOR ME? .............................................. 59
14. ROCK ON .......................................................................... 65
15. FRIENDSHIP—ICING ON THE CAKE .................................. 71
16. WOMEN OF INFLUENCE ................................................... 75
17. THE 4:13's—THE GIFTS OF JESUS ..................................... 79
18. PRAYER—IT IS A PRIVILEGE ............................................. 85
19. I AM THE I AM .................................................................. 89
20. FRET NOT THYSELF ........................................................... 95
21. BEING SURE .................................................................... 101
22. PRAYING GOD'S WORD . . . SPEAKING TO GOD WITH THE MOST BEAUTIFUL WORDS IN THE WORLD—HIS! ................................................................... 107
23. DON'T SWEAT THE SMALL STUFF .................................. 113
24. MARY, MARTHA AND ME ............................................... 119
25. FAN THE FLAME .............................................................. 125
26. GRACE! GRACE! GRACE! ................................................ 129
27. LISTEN TO YOUR COACH ............................................... 133
28. WORK IN PROGRESS ...................................................... 137

| 29. | DRESS FOR SUCCESS Part 1 | 141 |
| 30. | DRESS FOR SUCCESS Part 2 | 147 |
| 31. | DRESS FOR SUCCESS Part 3 | 153 |
| 32. | DON'T PUT GOD IN A BOX | 157 |
| 33. | SEEING IS BELIEVING | 163 |
| 34. | GLOBAL POSITIONING SYSTEM (G.P.S.) | 167 |
| 35. | WHEN UPSIDE DOWN MAKES SENSE | 173 |
| 36. | ME . . . A CLOSER LOOK ☺ | 177 |
| 37. | GOD 101 | 181 |
| 38. | GOD 102 | 187 |
| 39. | FAVOR ADDS FLAVOR | 193 |
| 40. | WHAT IS YOUR MESSAGE? | 199 |
| 41. | THE PURSUIT OF HAPPINESS | 205 |
| 42. | SMELLIN' LIKE A ROSE | 211 |
| 43. | YOUR MIND—DO YOUR THOUGHTS REALLY MATTER? | 217 |
| 44. | WOMEN FROM THE BIBLE—WOMEN JUST LIKE US? | 221 |
| 45. | PROMISES—HIS WORD IS TRUE | 227 |
| 46. | TO REJOICE IS A CHOICE | 231 |
| 47. | GIVE THANKS WITH A GRATEFUL HEART | 235 |
| 48. | GOOD THINGS | 239 |
| 49. | COMMONSENSE FROM PROVERBS | 245 |
| 50. | CHRISTMAS SELAH | 251 |
| 51. | "GLORY TO GOD IN THE HIGHEST . . ." | 257 |
| 52. | ANGELS | 263 |

| STEPS TO A NEW LIFE PLAN OF SALVATION | 269 |
| ANSWERS TO GOD 101 WORK SHEET | 271 |
| ABOUT THE AUTHOR | 273 |

*The grass withers; the flower fades, but the
word of God stands forever.*

Isaiah 40:8

# ABOUT THIS BOOK

This book of Bible studies can be a benefit if you study it by yourself; however you will also be blessed if you study with a few friends and share thoughts and experiences as you study God's word. Be sure to always include a time of prayer when you get together with your sisters. In this way you are inviting Jesus into the group and building unity.

These studies are designed to help you grow deeper in your relationship with Jesus Christ using different areas such as confidence, self-esteem, faith, grace, and friendship with your sisters in Christ.

My hope and prayer is that you use this book of studies to draw closer to the One who redeemed you to walk in victory. And that you don't just know Him in your head, but in your heart as well. Living on planet Earth is all about preparation for Heaven. You will be blessed when you journey through this short earthly life with sisters!

Blessings!

# 1

# AND THEN SOME

I'm not too big on New Year's resolutions, but usually at the start of a new year I start to think about how (and if) I have grown over the last year and what I need to do to become a kinder, selfless, more godly person this coming year. I visualize a scene where I arrive in Heaven after leaving this old world and see all the missed opportunities I could have been a part of—if only I had been more God focused and less me focused.

It's not that God wants me to work harder so I can live in Heaven with Him someday. Ephesians 2:8-9 says that *"For by grace you have been saved through faith, and that not of yourselves; it is the gift of God, ⁹ not of works, lest anyone should boast."* (NKJV) I know that one day I'll enjoy being with Father God in eternity not because of what I do, but because of what Jesus did for me on the cross. But when I ponder on all the loving things my Savior has done for me throughout this last year, I want to do my best for Him.

I read some time ago that Mary Kay Ash, founder of Mary Kay Cosmetics said that the difference between average people and successful people in the company was the fact that they did everything required of them **"and then some."** She was really talking about success in business, but we can see a spiritual application here as well.

That is going to be my goal for the coming year. I'm going to try to do what I believe God is calling me to do with an "and then some" attitude!

Probably most of us don't have the goal of being just average, doing what we can to get by. Only doing what is required and no more doesn't bring fulfillment or the deep sense of joy that comes from going the extra mile or doing the job "and then some." Being above average involves time and preparation, so it is not possible to become more than average in all areas of our lives. And if we could accomplish that feat, we would be a little hard to live with, don't you think?

People with a passion for a certain thing are most likely to put more time and effort in it than those who don't. When my sister and I were young, my mother wanted us to learn how to play the piano. We took lessons for a couple of years and practiced on the piano that graced our living room—when our mother nagged us! (She might have threatened us too, but I don't remember that!) Needless to say, I didn't have a passion for learning the piano.

One thing I enjoy doing now is baking cookies. (Maybe you could call it a passion.) I like to be by myself in the kitchen when it's quiet in the house and I have no timetable or no interruptions. I like to have the house smell like cookies when the family comes home. It's a welcoming smell and they know there's a treat waiting for them. And I like to give cookies to others, especially those who need a little lift. My granddaughter requests cookies whenever she comes home from college. Some people have said that I make good chocolate chip cookies, so you could say that I'm an above average cookie baker.

~What are some things you enjoy doing and are good at?

~What are some things you have a passion for?

~What are some things you have an interest in and would be willing to give an "and then some" effort to be better than average at doing it?

When we have a gift or skill that we are willing for God to use, there is no doubt in my mind that He will use it to help or encourage someone in need. Even if you aren't especially gifted in that area, but are willing, He will use you. I didn't start out baking wonderful cookies. They got to be pretty good only after I put time and effort into baking them just right. In fact, He even used the extra brown ones I baked one time. A woman I knew loved extra done cookies and I called her when I left the cookies in the oven too long and she was blessed by them! Hard to believe—but true!

Every one of us is gifted by God to serve the body of Christ. That's what the Bible teaches in—

1 Corinthians 12:7 and 1 Peter 4:10 Look at them now please.

As you can see, the gifts God has gifted us with are for the benefit of the whole body. If we don't use these gifts that God picked out especially for us, everyone loses. We are to use these gifts and develop and hone them because God has entrusted them to us. These gifts are given to us through the Holy Spirit living within us and they are as different and diverse and unique as each of us. And not only that, but the Holy Spirit empowers us to develop and use them. Now that's something to get passionate about!

Let's look at the different spiritual gifts found in Romans 12:6-8 and 1 Corinthians 12:8-10. List as many as you can find below.

1._____ 2._____ 3._____
4._____ 5._____ 6._____
7._____ 8._____ 9._____
10._____ 11._____ 12._____
13._____ 14._____ 15._____
16._____

If you know your gifts, circle them. Everyone has at least one. If you don't know your gifts, circle the ones you think would be a good fit for you. They would be the ones that you have an interest in or others have told you that you are good at.

It is important to us and also to our spiritual family to have this knowledge. This is one of the main ways that God will give you opportunities to work. Look at Galatians 6:10. Notice who we should be ministering to first.

Three of these spiritual gifts—serving, giving and showing mercy—are also commanded of us. Look at;

**SERVING**—Psalm 100:2; Ephesians 4:11-13; and Galatians 5:13.

To serve is to attend to, minister to, care for, help, be of use, assist, benefit, promote, support, make easy for, nourish, or encourage. I'm pretty sure that all of us do one or more of these activities. As godly women, we are called to serve. For some of us that role is where our comfort zone begins and ends. While it is a good place to be, God didn't leave us here on planet Earth to be comfortable. He wants us to be willing to stretch ourselves beyond our comfort level.

**GIVING**—Proverbs 3:27 and Luke 3:11.

The Word says that God loves a cheerful giver. It must be that our attitude is important to Him. Does it really mean anything if you give with a sour mind-set? Or a selfish one, thinking that one day you'll get paid back and more? No, this is where the "and then some" approach works the best. Because we are so blessed by God, we can respond by showing kindness and generosity to those who cross our paths.

The principle for giving is found in Luke 6:38 which says, *"Give, and it will be given to you; good measure, pressed down, shaken together, running over, it will be poured into your lap. For by your standard of measure it will be measured to you in return."* NIV

**SHOWING MERCY**—Matthew 5:7; Micah 6:8; and Luke 6:36.

Mercy is to show kindness, forgiveness, compassion, to show tender feelings, to understand and to give blessings to, to pardon, and not condemn.

When our hearts are in tune with Father God and we can see things through His eyes, we can show love and mercy to others in a way that we can never do in our natural state. It is a desirable ability to have and one we should ask the Father to help us develop. One way we can thank God for all He has done for us is to share His love and mercy with others.

**The great love of God is an ocean without a bottom or a shore. C.H. Spurgeon**

Whether you know and are currently using your spiritual gifts or not, these three gifts are for each one of us to practice and you know what they say about practice! ☺ If we are willing to use these three general gifts, don't you think that God will give us opportunities to use other spiritual gifts that are uniquely ours?

As we grow and mature in our faith, we find that changes occur. What was once important to us is now not such a big deal. We look at people and things in a new light. Where we once called our girlfriends when we needed advice, now we first turn to God. We are growing into strong, confident women because we know Who we belong to. We are always learning through prayer, Bible study, and being with our sisters in the faith. We are each learning God's purpose and plan for us and we can say no to the things that don't fit into that plan. And we are doing all this with an "and then some" attitude.

Is God blessed? Yes!

Are we blessed beyond measure? Yes!

Blessings!

# 2

# ORGANIZATION—HOW IS THIS A SPIRITUAL MATTER?

Time is a very valuable commodity. Have you ever found yourself wishing there were more than 24 hours in a day? Everyone has wished that at one time or another. But there is a way to achieve more in our 24 hours and that is to begin to see and do things in an organized way.

Ephesians 5:15-17 . . .
*"Look carefully then how you walk! Live purposefully and worthily and accurately, not as the unwise and witless, but as wise (sensible, intelligent people). Making the most of the time (buying up each opportunity), because the days are evil. Therefore do not be vague and thoughtless and foolish, but understanding and firmly grasping what the will of the Lord is."* AMP

What do you think scripture means by the phrase *"walk carefully"*?

What are every day practical ways to *"live purposeful, worthily and accurately"*?

What does it mean when it says *"because the days are evil"*?

How can we understand and firmly grasp what the will of the Lord is concerning our lives?

Ask God to teach you to live wisely. Pay attention to the way you spend your time and make the most of every opportunity. You can be sure that praying for wisdom and opportunities are prayers that God will honor in your life.

We must guard our time daily. The following are some of the time-robbers that creep into our daily lives. Put a check by the ones that are robbing you.

1. Procrastination
2. Poor planning and scheduling
3. People not on the plan for the day
4. Poor delegation
5. Poor use of the phone
6. Poring over junk mail and newspapers
7. Priorities out of whack

If you've made up your mind to recapture your time, bring those that you have checked to the Lord before you go to bed tonight.

John 9:4 . . .
*"I must work the works of Him who sent Me while it is day; the night is coming when no one can work."* NKJV

If we can manage our homes, work, and lives in an organized way, then we have more time to be about our Father's business. Focus on the eternal, not the temporal.

If you adopted John 9:4 as your life verse (one which you live by daily) what in your life would have to change?

When you think about your use of time, which statement best describes your thoughts?

1. I'm totally disorganized!
2. I'm trying hard—but I never catch up.
3. I'm not getting anything important done.
4. I've got a pretty good handle on my time.
5. You wouldn't believe how far behind I am.
6. I feel like I'm on a never-ending rat race.

7. Fill in blank _____.

In order to be able to say "I've got a pretty good handle on my time." What could you do to overcome what's interfering with the best use of your time?

Read these scriptures to find instructions God's Word gives about use of time. Summarize the instructions in a short phrase or sentence.

Proverbs 10:4-5

Ephesians 5:15-16

Colossians 3:23

2 Corinthians 6:1-2

Hebrews 3:13

2 Thessalonians 3:11-15

## DON'T JUST BE BUSY, BE FRUITFUL

Here are some ideas for saving time that I have gleaned from magazines and ones I have found that work for me. Start with prayer and commit your day to the Lord. If you pray "Father, help me manage the things You bring into my life today with a confidence and calmness that honors You."

Add to that prayer, *"Let the words of my mouth and the meditations of my heart be acceptable to You, O Lord."* (Psalm 19:14 NASB)

1. SPEED DUSTING: Take an old sock, put it on your left hand, spray with furniture cleaner, and you're ready to dust. Use your right hand to pick up things that need to be put away or thrown away.
2. COMPUTER KEYBOARD: Dust with a large clean makeup brush or paint brush. To clean the keys, wipe with a soft cloth dampened

lightly with glass cleaner. The brush idea works well on lots of things aren't a smooth, flat surface.

3. CLOGGED SHOWER HEAD: If you can't remove it, pour vinegar into a sandwich bag and attach it to the shower-head with a rubber band for an overnight soak. It's pretty amazing how good it works in the morning!

4. LOOKING GOOD: Find a hairstyle that fits your lifestyle. Low-maintenance if you're busy (and who isn't) and get a trim every 5-6 weeks.

5. COSMETICS: Keep all the cosmetics you use every morning in one place—on a shelf, in a clear organizer or plastic zippered bag—so that you don't have to think about what to reach for. Keep duplicates in your purse or where you work.

6. TWO THINGS AT ONCE: While you're supervising a child's evening bath, give yourself a facial, tweeze your eyebrows, or do your pre-bed beauty routine. Look for other things you can double up on.

7. BE PREPARED: Anything you can prepare at night seems to save hours in the morning—especially lunches and clothes. Have the children chose their clothes for the next day. Good idea for you and husband too. (This is really good advice for Sunday morning, because we all know the devil works overtime then.)

8. SHOPPING: Never buy just one of anything you use often, such as tuna, shampoo, or cans of soup. Especially if it's on sale and you have room to store it. You'd spend the money on it eventually.

9. STYLE: Never buy an incomplete outfit. Make certain you already own something to wear with the new purchase, or buy the extra piece at the same time.

10. TELEPHONE: If the phone rings when you are in the middle of something, let the answering machine get it and return the calls at a more convenient time. To end a phone conversation promptly, try one of these ideas: Don't ask, "How are you?" Say, "What can I do for you?" or say, "I can't talk right now, when would be a good time to call you back?"

11. JUNK MAIL: Don't read it, toss it!

12. MESSAGES: Keep notepaper and pencil next to the phone so you don't waste your time and the caller's time searching for something to write a message on. Very important if you are on the prayer chain!

13. LISTS: Never run errands without a list. Make a circle of the stops you need to make so you don't have to backtrack. Make a Six Most Important Things to Do List every night so you have a head start on the next day. List your most important phone numbers for your purse. Also program them into your cell phone. List your medications and those of your family on your computer so you can easily take a copy to the doctor's office for a quick reference. Your various lists can go on and on . . . being organized with a list reduces stress.
14. The average wait in a doctor's office is 23.4 minutes. Plan ahead. Take a book, your knitting, your day planner, etc. Not only will you feel that you've accomplished something, you'll be less stressed.

What are some other time-savers that have worked for you? Share if you will.

There are many ways to manage your day and to retrieve some of the time wasters that seem to be a part of every day. Keep your eyes open for ways to reduce your stress level and still take good care of your home and family. Discover small changes that will help you function better. ALLOW GOD TO BE IN the details of your day. Practice being in His presence as you do the necessary things to make your home and life run smooth. Doing that will add richness to the quality of your life.

Blessings!

# 3

# AM I MY SISTER'S KEEPER?

We are sisters. Look around. These are your sisters. Some of us are fortunate to have blood sisters. We are sisters to all women. It's called "The Sisterhood of Womanhood." (I just made that up.) We even have our own language. (I didn't make that up.) We speak it every day. It involves not having to finish our own sentences because the woman we are talking to already knows what we are going to say, before we say it. Men don't understand this. That's O.K. It's for sisters only.

Some of our sisters don't have a personal relationship with our Lord and Savior, Jesus Christ. Some sisters have met Him, but aren't growing in that relationship like God wants for all of us. Years ago, God began to give me new opportunities to serve Him and to minister to my sisters. It began with small group Bible studies. It was fun and exciting and I learned a lot about myself as I prepared for those studies. I saw other women growing as well as we got into the Word and shared insights about what we learned.

After a while, God gave me another blessed opportunity—disciplining new believers on a one on one basis. Discipleship simply means learning to follow Jesus. Learning the basics of Christian living and passing it on to a "babe" in Christ. The Bible compares the new believer to a new baby, but then immediately commands that the "babe" <u>grow up!</u>

Look at Ephesians 4:11-16 for further insight: Discuss or write down any thoughts you might have.

One might think how can I help others to grow in their faith when I have so much more growing to do myself. One thing I know and that is the teacher always benefits more than the student. We have to know it to teach it and that causes us to study! Sometimes we can be teaching others without even realizing it. It is surprising how much of an example we can be just being ourselves, doing our daily things. Because others may be watching and learning from us, we must make sure our spirits are sweet and our actions godly! Hard some days I know!

It's a fascinating, interesting, joyful adventure as we take this spiritual journey and if we are fortunate enough to take others along with us, the rewards will be greater than we can ever imagine!

There are only 2 things on this planet earth that are eternal—God's Word and people. So when we are studying and sharing God's Word with a friend, the time spent is preserved forever.

Think back to the time you made that life changing commitment to accept Jesus Christ as Lord and Savior of your life. What a joy, what a thrilling experience. Whether your conversion was as dramatic as Paul's on the road to Damascus or as quietly calm and reserved as Lydia's was as she sat there by the river, God entered our lives and began to abide with us and that began our spiritual journey.

And it's been a bed of roses ever since! No, of course not. Roses have thorns. We all experienced rocky places in our lives.

Who has been your encouragers over the years? Your mentors? Your teachers? Who has prayed with you and for you?

Please write some of those names down below:

1.

2.

3.

4.

Many of the names you've written down you may consider being saints of the church. But did you know that if you are a child of God, then you are a saint? Paul calls all Christians, saints in Romans 1:7 and in Romans 8:27 he writes... *"And He who searches our hearts knows the mind of the Spirit, because the Spirit intercedes for the saints (us) in accordance with God's will."* NIV

As you look back over your list, think of others, maybe newer in the faith that you could be an encourager to, that you could teach and pray with and be a friend to walk along side.

Make a second list with the names of those women:

1.

2.

3.

4.

Look next at these verses:

2 Timothy 2:15

1 Timothy 4:8

We know that being a godly woman is what God wants us to be and from the verses we just read, we know godliness is a good thing for us, both now and into eternity. But how can we train ourselves to be godly?

Look at Colossians 4:2-6. There are 3 things here that God is telling us to do:

## ~ DEVOTE YOURSELF TO PRAYER

Have time alone with God everyday (TAWG). Do you think that busyness is a sin? It could be if it keeps us from having TAWG. If our days are so filled, we can't set aside time for God, then we have 2 choices:

1. Get up 15 minutes earlier
2. Remove something from your agenda and replace it with an appointment with God.

Jealously guard this time, because it will strengthen you for the rest of the day. This will be the time when the phone rings or the washer overflows or one of many other unexpected things, but don't give up! Use this time with God to: pray (for yourself and others), praise, listen, meditate and memorize scripture.

If you have daily time with God, share how the experience has benefited you and how you've managed to keep this time reserved. Following are 5 ideas that might rejuvenate your prayer life:

1. Use a prayer journal to write your requests, and date them. Also record the answered prayer. You'll be blessed again as you read them years from now.
2. Write out your prayers. Sometimes we can express ourselves more clearly and sometimes we see situations differently when we see it written out.
3. Pray in a different place—outside, maybe in your backyard
4. Begin your prayer time with praise choruses. Songs can sometimes express more heartfelt worship then our own words.
5. Have a trusted prayer partner or join (or start) a small group that meets regularly. There is power in a group of people praying.

## ~ CLEARLY KNOW WHAT YOU BELIEVE

The second thing we need to do as godly women is to know and speak clearly the word of God. To be confident in our speech, we need to know our Bibles. The time reading it and studying it is time well spent.

God reveals Himself to us through His word. We come to know Him and what He expects of us through reading and hearing and studying His word. One of the things He expects of us is to share our faith with others.

When we read and study God's word, we begin to formulate in our minds what we believe and when we know what we believe about God, Jesus, salvation, eternal life, then we have the confidence to speak to others about spiritual things. Time is too short not to be about our Father's business!

## ~ BE GRACIOUS AND WISE IN CONDUCT

The third thing Col. 4 instructs us to do as godly women and disciples of Jesus is found in verses 5-6: *"Conduct yourselves with wisdom toward outsiders making the most of every opportunity. Let your speech always be with grace, seasoned as it were with salt, so that you may know how you should respond to each person."* NASB

Look back to your list of encouragers and teachers that have helped you along your spiritual journey. Weren't they wise, gracious, always saying the right thing?

We as sisters in the "Sisterhood of the Faith" (made it up) need to be on the look out for our baby sisters who need us to walk along beside them. When God nudges you toward a sister, go. Remember, blessings always follow obedience!

(Visual Demonstration)

This is a rubber band. What is its purpose?

**WE MUST BE LIKE RUBBER BANDS. WILLING TO BE STRETCHED AND USED TO HELP OTHERS STRETCH.**

YOU NEVER KNOW
You never know when someone
May catch a dream from you.
You never know when a little word
Or something you may do
May open up the windows
Of a mind that seeks the light . . .
The way you live may not matter at all
But you never know . . . it might.
And just in case it could be
That another's life, through you,

Might possibly change for the better
With a broader and brighter view,
It seems it might be worth a try
At pointing the way to the right . . .
Of course, it may not matter at all,
But then again . . . it might.
Author unknown

Blessings!

# 4

# GROWING IN FAITH TOGETHER
## Part 1

**"Living by faith is one of the most normal activities of human existence."**

Do you agree or disagree? Why?

Name some things that we believe every day that are on the basis of somebody else's word. Here's one to get you started:

1. *weather man*
2.
3.
4.
5.

All of these are daily sources of information or opinion which we believe. They influence our attitudes, emotions and sometimes how we dress. These all are some form of believing, trusting, or exercising faith in some source. Sometimes we put our faith in something or someone that is not trustworthy. You can see why it is important to go to a source that has been proven reliable.

We are intended to live by faith. Our Christian faith is based on a proved trustworthy source—God's Holy Word.

What does Proverbs 30:5 say about God's Word?

Isaiah 40:8 describes the reason we can trust God's Word. What does it say?

Before we *can grow* in our faith walk, we must make the decision *to begin* our faith walk by taking God at His word and claim His salvation by faith.

In Acts 16:30-31 what did the Philippian jailer ask Paul and Silas?

That act of believing and accepting God's gift of salvation is the beginning point of our faith. But God does not want us to remain as babies in our faith walk. He has a plan and purpose for us. What does 2 Peter 3:18 tell us?

When we fail to grow spiritually, we do ourselves a great disservice and miss countless blessings. Instead, we should desire to grow each day and taste the abundant life Jesus talked about in John 10:10. I don't know about you, but I want all that God offers now and in eternity!

God wants us to grow to the point that one of our first thoughts each morning in our hearts is about how you can bless someone else today. You heard the saying, "You can't take it with you." Well you can take people. That's one of God's purposes for us as we live this short time on planet Earth.

To be spiritually mature is to show the fruit of the Spirit in our lives.

Write the 9 areas of fruit below and then check in Galatians 5:22-23 to see if you've remembered them.

1.   2.   3.   4.

5.   6.   7.   8.

9.

What area do you need to work on?

What area comes easy for you?

If you're not satisfied with yourself in these areas, (and you shouldn't be, ever!) ask God to help you. This is a prayer that God would be delighted to answer for you. And remember; don't be afraid to go out on a limb, because that's where the good fruit is!

Faith is the most important element in our Christian walk. The Bible says that without faith you cannot please God. Our faith can start small. God is more interested in the sincerity of our hearts. There is a story in Matthew 17:20 about a mustard seed of faith being able to move a mountain.

If you've ever seen a mustard seed, you know how tiny it is. In Jesus' day the mustard seed was a symbol of anything tiny or insignificant. The point here is even an insignificant faith can move mountains, because the power of faith is not in the strength of our belief but in the strength of the One in whom we believe.

We are all in different stages of our faith walk. Some of us are beginning; some of us have been faithful for a long time, and others some where in the middle, but we are all walking in faith together, learning from each other, growing together. We need the encouragement we receive from one another to continue growing.

In Luke 18:17 we read that Jesus said: *"whoever does not receive the Kingdom of God like a child shall not enter it at all."* (NASB) He was telling us that our faith should have child-like qualities. What are some of those qualities? Why would those character traits be good in our lives?

That is not to say that we should remain "baby" Christians. Look at Hebrews 5:12-14. Maturity comes with practice. The spiritual principles we learn must also be lived out in our lives.

Two important things that we need to keep in mind as we are walking and growing in our faith:

1. We don't have to walk alone. We need the support and encouragement of others and they need us too. Growing in faith together. It makes for a more joyful journey!

2. Discovering God's faithfulness to you as an individual will add to your faith. God, the Creator of the Universe, loves you. He desires that you have a blessed and fulfilled life here on planet Earth as you are preparing to spend eternity with Him.

Look at Hebrews 11:1

Write your definition of faith here:

Blessings!

# 5

# GROWING IN FAITH TOGETHER
## Part 2

If Jesus returned today and found us just the way we are, He would not be disappointed in us as long as we are striving to grow and become more like the Father desires us to be. We are a work in progress.

Philippians 1:6:
*"Being confident of this, that He who began a good work in you will carry it on to completion until the day of Christ Jesus."* (NIV)

This verse is a promise to us. God's part is the Holy Spirit's guiding, convicting and convincing work in our lives. Our part is to let God's love and the Holy Spirit's work shine in our lives and spill onto others as we influence the people in the world around us.

How can our Christian faith be increased? Maybe you've heard the notion that faith is a muscle and if you don't use it you lose it. The more time and effort that we put into growing our faith, the more we grow. Consistent study of God's Word and a regular time of communion with Him is essential. Christian fellowship would also seem to be necessary. Look up the following scriptures and discuss how they help and encourage us in the faith. Write down the things that jump out at you that might be meaningful in growing your faith.

James 1:2-4

1 Peter 1:6-7

2 Peter 1:5-8

Romans 10:14-15

Hebrews 10:23

Hebrews 10:24-25

Hebrews 11:6

What about doubts? Some of these things we've discussed aren't that simple in real life. It isn't always easy to prevail when you are in pain or your child is in trouble or you can't stand your neighbor, let alone tell him about Jesus. Doubts will come at various times and due to a variety of reasons. Keep the following things in mind:

1. When you are near the end of your "faith rope", go back to Hebrews 11:6 and claim it. We must believe that "God rewards those who earnestly seek Him."
2. Place your unwavering assurance in the clear truth of God's Word.
3. Ask for the Holy Spirit's guidance. Listen carefully and follow His leading.
4. Don't quit. Don't. Ever.

### *FAITH MAKES THINGS POSSIBLE—IT DOES NOT MAKE THEM EASY.*

In the 1600's there lived a monk of the Carmelite Order in Paris who's name was Brother Lawrence. He was a man of humble beginnings who discovered the greatest secret of living in the Kingdom of God here on earth. It is the art of "practicing the presence of God in one single act that does not end." His thoughts and writings are in a book called, "THE PRACTICE OF THE

PRESENCE OF GOD." He felt that the essential practices for the spiritual life are to have a running conversation with God while we go about the business of the day. And rather than pray a memorized prayer, just talk to God from our hearts.

OK, I know he was a monk and didn't have the daily responsibilities that we who live in a busy, fast-paced world do, but his ideas are certainly ones that we could adapt to fit into our lives, don't you think?

Brother Lawrence wrote that praise is good. As we are working along, we should stop for a few minutes and praise God for whatever comes to our hearts and that way we would enjoy a more intimate relationship with Father God.

These may be some of the things you already do in your daily life, but they remind us to bring God into everything we do. He wants to be involved in our lives and we have the benefit of His presence!

Brother Lawrence also wrote that **"when we begin our Christian walk, we must remember that we have been living in the world, subject to all sorts of miseries, accidents, and poor dispositions from within. The Lord will cleanse and humble us in order to make us more like Christ. As we go through this cleansing process, we will grow closer to God. Therefore, we should rejoice in our difficulties bearing them as long as the Lord wills because only through such trials will our faith become purified, more precious than gold."** (See 1 Peter 1:7, 4:19)

We need to get to the point in our faith walk that the first thought every morning is of God and crave His presence.

Look at:

Isaiah 26:9a

Psalm 42:1

Knowing about water doesn't satisfy your thirst—drinking water does. Knowing about God doesn't satisfy the emptiness you feel in your soul, actually being in God's presence does.

Don't think this is an impossible goal to obtain. We will be blessed for trying. God will be blessed for us trying. God is always blessed when we put Him first.

When God in His fiery presence descended from heaven to meet Moses on Mount Sinai, He delivered a document citing ten basic rules for His people to live by, the most important being *"You shall have no other gods before me."* (see Exodus 20)

This statement was a complete change in the customs of the day. All other nations worshiped many gods. But God's chosen people, the children of Israel, were to establish a nation that would be a light to the world, showing others the joy that comes when people live in accordance with the design and purpose of our loving Creator, the one true God, who formed us in His own image.

Years later, Moses explained the first commandment. Having no other god but God means loving Him with every aspect of our being—heart, soul, and strength (see Deut. 6:5). To love God means having a relationship with Him that is so full and satisfying that it slowly crowds out all other desires, habits, thoughts or actions.

Look at the Ten Commandments found in Exodus 20:3-17

Notice that all these commands are about relationships. The first 4 are about our relationship with God. The last 6 concern our relationship with each other.

All the commandments can be covered under one theme—love. Look at Romans 13:8-10 and Matthew 22:34-40.

Knowing about the commandments and living them are two different things. We can show our love to God by our obedience. The things He requires of us are always for our own good and well fare. We will always be blessed when we do things God's way.

Blessings!

# 6

# WITH ALL MY HEART

The question was asked of Jesus, *"Of all the commandments, which is the most important?"* (Matthew 22:36) This was His answer:

*"You shall love the LORD your God with all your heart, with all your soul, and with all your mind."* Matthew 22:37NKJV

Doesn't this sound like God wants our entire being?

The heart is an organ which by its action keeps the blood in circulation. Good news for us since that is how we have physical life. The heart also has come to stand for the center of moral, intellectual and spiritual life. Take a look at Luke 6:45.

Where does this verse say that our actions come from?

Just as we know how important it is to keep our heart healthy for our physical well being, we should also look after our hearts to be spiritually healthy.

Our passion while we are here on planet Earth should be to worship God with our whole being. After all, He is the one who created us. He is the one responsible for everything we see, hear, smell, and touch. Our passion needs to be stirred up every now and then. A good way to do that is to look in the

Psalms. King David and the other writers there seemed to know how to put words to the deep feelings we can't express. Look at these verses and see if these words speak to your deepest love for God:

Psalm 9:1-2

Psalm 18:1-3

Psalm 28:6-7

Psalm 42:1

Unfortunately, this heartfelt, loving attitude is not the norm. He gave us the right to choose and all too often we choose not to give our best back to Him. When we fail to give God proper reverence and honor, we are disrespecting Him. He doesn't want our leftovers. Malachi 1:7 says that his people *"offered defiled food on My altar."* Don't we as modern day believers, do that when we worship Him in a half-hearted way?

What are some ways that we worship God in a less than honoring, half-hearted way?

In church services:

In private, every day circumstances:

Oh! But let's not give up on us yet. God hasn't! There is a little chorus that starts out, "I'll say yes, Lord, yes to Your will and to Your way . . ." When we do surrender our will to His, then our worship and praise of Him is natural and genuine and shows in our daily lives.

I believe it all begins with our heart attitude. How deep is our love and gratitude to our Father God? Do we know and have we experienced His love to us? If so, have we forgotten the things He has provided for us? Do we take God for granted? If we do then our commitment level is not where it's supposed to be.

The fact is that we all have answered in the negative to these questions if we've been honest. Thankfully we have an understanding Heavenly Father who is full of mercy and grace and is ready and waiting to give us a second chance. He wants our all. He wants a heart that is totally committed to Him.

Those are the hearts and lives that He can use. And what blessings come from being used by God!

Let's look to the Word to remind us why we should give to God our whole hearts.

Psalm 95:1-2 . . . Why should we come before our God with thanksgiving and joyful shouts?

Psalm 95:3-4 . . . Doesn't this verse remind us that God is everywhere? Know any other that can say that?

Psalm 95:4-5 . . . Have you ever been out on the ocean or even a big lake where you can't see land? Have you been in the mountains and seen down into the valley or seen another mountain in the way off distance?

Psalm 95:6 . . . Does seeing the awesome things God has created make you want to worship Him? How about when you look in the mirror?

Psalm 95:7 . . . Do you ever wonder why we are compared to sheep? Sheep are the most helpless animal around. Thankfully, we have a Shepherd who desires to take care of us. When you think of His infinite care in your life, how does it make you feel?

Psalm 8 . . . When we look around us and see all the beauty He created for us to live in, what emotions do you feel? And to think after all this, He made us too and He made us in His own image! How awesome!

We all know of people, who after they've accepted Jesus into their heart, their lives seem to be on fire! Jesus is all they talk about. Even strangers hear how the Lord is working in their lives and blessing them daily. It's exciting to hear them talk about the Lord! Soon though, the fire dies down and sometimes even goes out.

Why? You ask. Why does this happen to some and not others? Sometimes it may be the fear of drawing to close to God. He may ask you to give up every creature comfort and be a missionary to Africa. It may be that one is struggling with doubt. Oh sure, my relationship with God started out great but how can it possibly last? The problem might be impatience or laziness. To grow a lasting relationship takes time and work. Those are all excuses to not making the right choice.

What sometimes is not realized in the beginning of a relationship with God is the life long blessings and opportunities that will be missed if our commitment level isn't there.

What can we do if we find ourselves not being able to fill that God sized hole that is born in everyone?

~First make a list of every reason you can think of for not giving your whole heart to Him.

~Next, make every reason a matter of prayer. Ask God to release you from these barriers. Of course, He can do it. He's God, after all!

~Then find scriptures to help you to release all your misgivings and doubts.

~Practice the truths and principles you find in the scriptures. Make the changes you need to make in your everyday life. Determine with all your heart to be faithful to the only One who is worthy of your faithfulness.

You'll find that all you need to do is take that first step of faith and God will be right there with you. He is the God who never casts out or drives away those who come to him. (see John 6:37) He comes near those who draw near to Him. (see James 4:8) He is a rewarder of those who diligently seek Him. (see Heb. 11:6)

Today is the best day to make a determination, a commitment, a choice to really know God. Give Him your best. Give Him your whole heart, mind, soul and strength. Then joyfully live out your life here in planet Earth until the day He welcomes you home.

Psalm 32:11 *"Be glad in the Lord and rejoice you (uncompromisingly) righteous (you who are upright and in right standing with Him); shout for joy, all you upright in heart!"* AMP

Blessings!

# 7

# ABOVE ALL

*"Above all things have intense and unfailing love for one another, for love covers a multitude of sins (forgives and disregards the offenses of others.)"* 1 Peter 4:8 AMP.

It's pretty easy, isn't it, to love those who love you and act lovingly toward you. But to have a love for someone who has offended you? Not so much. And to love that person with an intense love? Hard to do and impossible to achieve except for the indwelling of the Holy Spirit in our lives. But that's what God is telling us to do in this verse.

God doesn't tell us to do anything He knows we are not capable of. But because He planted the seed of love in us, (one of the fruit of the Spirit) He expects us to grow and nurture that seed of love until it becomes a habit in our lives.

Think of someone right now that makes you annoyed, frustrated, upset, angry, or even downright boiling mad. Now think of that person through God's focus. God loves that person just as much as He loves you. Seems unfair doesn't it? Oh, He doesn't love the offense the person committed against you, but He loves the person just the same. He sent His Son to die for that person the same as He did for you.

It is certainly a hard pill to swallow, but thinking that God's love extends to that person as well as you might put things in proper perspective. I believe forgiving offenses is more for our benefit than the offender. Forgiving sets you free. Anyone can love the people who love and accept them. The harder thing is to love those who rub you the wrong way or maybe lie or gossip about you. We can only love those people the supernatural way—through the love that God has for us.

Look at Luke 6:32 for more insight.

Do you have a difficult person in your life? How are you dealing with that person? Is accepting that person easier when you know God loves that person as much as He loves you?

When you realize how much God loves you—with an extravagant, irresistible, unconditional love, then His love will change your entire focus on life. If we don't receive His love for us, we'll have a hard time loving the unlovely, the difficult, and the irritable people who are difficult or demanding.

Fortunately, most people in our lives are friendly and loving and not difficult at all. But it just takes one irritable person to challenge our positive outlook and spoil our day.

Let's not kid ourselves. Love is tough to achieve sometimes. Sometimes it's a rocky road and as hard as you may try, you may have no warning of its unpredictability, like the young man in this story:

**The young suitor was determined to win the heart of the girl he wanted to marry, in spite of her rejection of his proposals a number of times.**

**He began what can only be called "campaigning" and sent her a small token of his affection every day for a month to her house.**

**Soon, the young lady fell in love with the UPS man.**

Neither should love be taken lightly. Relationships we make on planet Earth need to be nurtured and considered precious. In all of our relationships the other person's needs should be well thought-out. Here's another story to illustrate how quickly we can underestimate its importance:

**A friend and his wife were considering traveling to Alaska for a trip that the husband had long dreamed of taking. He kept talking about how great it would be to stay in a log cabin without electricity, to hunt moose, and drive a dog team instead of a car.**

**"If we decided to live there permanently, away from civilization, what would you miss the most?" he asked his wife. She replied, "You."**

Those are just two small examples of how the building of relationships can go wrong. We are a funny people here on planet Earth. Good thing we've got a Heavenly Father who can give us wisdom when we ask.

By learning to love others with the love God gives you, you will have a greater influence with that person and it may lead to spiritual things. When you make a habit of loving others regardless of the circumstances, you will experience love as God means it to be, filled with joy.

It's true, isn't it, that difficult people will zap your energy and rob your joy? Refuse to allow this to happen! Love them back, show them kindness instead of an angry response. At the very least, it will confuse them! But at the most, you may win them for Christ!

The Bible speaks of three types of love: God's love for us, our love for God, and our love for each other. In 1 John 4:8 it states that, *"God is love."* Love is rooted in the very essence of Him. Many times in the Word it describes God's love as endless, boundless or enduring. His greatest expression of love is in John 3:16 which says, *"For God so greatly loved and dearly prized the world that He gave up His only begotten, unique Son, so that whoever believes in (trusts in, clings to, relies on) Him shall not perish (come to destruction, be lost) but have eternal (everlasting) life."* AMP.

Our love for God comes in response to the gratitude we feel for this act of love, which we did nothing to obtain. This gratitude we feel to God for this remarkable act of kindness and grace moves us to show love toward one another. And if we love in the way God desires us to love, we can not only direct our love to our family and friends but to strangers and even our enemies as well.

Look at these verses that talk about God's love. Give a short description of each.

Romans 5:8

Romans 8: 38-39

Psalm 99:5

**"God loves each of us as if there were only one of us." St. Augustine**

There are many more verses that talk about God's love for us. As an expression of our love for Him, we should pause each day and ask God to show us how to share our love for everyone we meet. People need to know they are loved and accepted. It is amazing how a smile and a little kindness can change the day for someone who is having a bad day.

See Matthew 25:35-40 and discuss the lesson there.

A wise person once said, "Pretend every person you meet has a sign on them that says . . . I AM SPECIAL and treat them according." That should be easy if we remember that verse and treat people as if you would be treating Jesus. How would your daily life change if you adopted this principle?

God is very concerned about how we relate to other people because He wants us to love them. We are His hands and feet here on planet Earth. When we walk through our day with thoughts of others and their needs, it will give us an open door when they have questions concerning spiritual matters. Ephesians 4:1 says to *"walk worthy of the calling you have received"* and in verse 2 it tells us to *"bear with one another in love."* Our faith walk should be a love walk.

How many of us believe we are blessed? I believe there is a reason we are blessed and the reason is so we can bless others. Sometimes being a blessing costs time and/or money. Sometimes it just costs us a smile. But no matter what the cost to us, in the bigger picture, we are the ones who are blessed. Being a blessing to others brings to our lives—joy, peace, and fulfillment and lots of other positive things. And it blesses God when His children find ways to be a blessing to others.

A life principle is that you reap what you sow. If you encourage people, you will get encouragement when you need it. If you are friendly to all you meet, you will never be without friends. If you are quick to forgive offenses, you will find forgiveness. If you are faithful to pray for others needs, your needs will be prayed for as well. If you want a blessed life, be a blessing.

Above all, we want to honor God. The more we demonstrate love and kindness to others, the more we become like Him. That is a benefit to our relationship with Him and strengthens our prayer life. Be a reflection of God's love and in doing so you may be the pathway for others to find salvation through His Son, Jesus Christ.

People before things;
People before projects;
Family before friends;
Husband before children;
Husband before parents;
Tithe before wants;
Bible before opinions;
Jesus before all.
Author unknown

Blessings!

# 8

# WORDS OF LIFE

You and I will have many choices through-out our lives. Even daily in our thought life there are choices to make. It's amazing how our days can begin so good and then without much effort; our minds wander over into worldly, fleshly, wrong thinking.

One might think it's okay if we think negative thoughts as long as we don't say it out loud. But our thoughts tend to become our words. That's why it's important to choose life-giving thoughts.

Look in Deuteronomy 30:19 and see what God told the Jewish people. Write it out here:

Life or death, blessings or curses, heaven or hell—our choices now will make the difference in where we will spend eternity and not only that (all though that's a big deal!) our choices determine our abundant life living out our allotted time on this planet Earth.

Look at Proverbs 18:21. Write it here:

Our words are powerful. They can help or hurt. They can encourage or discourage. Not only do our words affect those around us, but they affect us too. When we speak positive, life-giving words, they are coming from a positive mind set. How can we have the right heart attitude if we think and speak negatively? How can we glorify God when we have the wrong heart attitude?

Proverbs 25:11 says, *"A word fitly spoken and in due season is like apples of gold in settings of silver."* AMP

What does the phase *"in due season"* mean?

Instead of *"apples of gold in settings of silver"*, describe a "modern-day treasure".

What would a word in due season do for a person who is hurting?

Have you ever received such a blessing? Share if you will.

Our words have value. They can improve a situation or circumstance. Isaiah 50:4 tells us that speaking words in due season to one another will keep us from growing weary.

## PRAISE LOUDLY . . . BLAME SOFTLY.

Another verse that we can use to guide us in our speech is written in Ephesians 4:29. Look at it here from the AMP:

*"Let no foul or polluting language, or evil word nor unwholesome or worthless talk (ever) come out of your mouth, but only such (speech) as is good and beneficial to the spiritual progress of others, as is fitting to the need and the occasion, that it may be a blessing and give grace (God's favor) to those who hear it."*

A few weeks ago, John and I were having lunch at a local restaurant. What should have been a nice time with my husband was spoiled for me because of the un-wholesome, polluting language coming from the table next to us.

These were obviously not Christian people who didn't have a clue that they were being a curse not a blessing. Because we live in the world, we'll often have situations like this. The best we can do is to try to not let it upset us and pray for the person to find Jesus. Have you had a similar experience? How did you handle it?

Matthew 12:34b says, *"For out of the abundance of the heart, the mouth speaks."* NKJV

If we allow wrong thoughts and attitudes to dwell within us, they will eventually come out in our speech. Whatever is hidden will sooner or later come forth.

Look at Matthew 12:36-37.

Now that you know that you are accountable to God for every word that comes out of your mouth, how will that change the way you talk?

We need to be so careful to love and encourage with our words. This includes our husbands and children as well. The home is a place where character and integrity is formed in young children. How we speak to them and about them can build their self—confidence. It also influences how their children are raised.

Remember the saying **"sticks and stones may break my bones, but words can never hurt me."** That is just not true. Words can hurt whether they were purposely meant to hurt or through careless talk. Negative words spoken to a child will be remembered long after childhood is over.

Look at Psalm 19:14.

This is a favorite scripture of mine and one I try to remember to pray every morning. If our thoughts and our mouths are pleasing to God, then they will certainly bring blessings to those we are around every day. It is amazing how good my day goes when I have prayed this scripture when I first wake up!

Here are two more verses having to do with words: look at Proverbs 15:1 and Proverbs 25:15.

We've probably all been in situations where someone says something to us that could be taken two ways. In that next few seconds, we have a choice to make—either reply in anger or respond with calmness and gentleness or maybe even humor.

The first choice will only get us more angry words in return and certainly not be God-honoring in any way. The second choice (to reply with calmness) will change the situation and stop an argument. It's no fun to argue with someone who won't fight back.

As women we enjoy getting the last word, but let that last word be healing, restoring, and uplifting. Proverbs 15:4 says that, *"A wholesome tongue is the tree of life,"* (NKJV) Let us never say things that will tear others down or be a discouragement to them. Our words can be carriers of either life or death. We choose life! Words are powerful. Take them seriously!

Don't you love people who complain? Moses must have been in his glory as he led three million or so people out of Egypt. Because of their complaining, God made an eleven day trip last for forty years. He wanted them to learn a few things.

It seems to me that the lesson we can learn from this Bible account (found in the book of Exodus) is that complaining slows down our break through, our answers to prayer and our spiritual growth. And on top of that, it certainly hurts our Christian witness. We are God's children, heirs to the King, forgiven, bought and paid for by the blood of Jesus Christ. We've nothing to complain about!

Turn to Philippians 2:14-16.

Do you ever wonder if the way you live your life is making a difference in the world around you?

These verses encourage us to shine as bright lights in a dark world. How bright is your light shining? Dear sisters, when we shine like stars, our world will be brighter, we'll be happier and more pleasant to be around and maybe in the process, we can introduce someone to our friend, Jesus!

Blessings!

# 9

# SHHH! LISTEN . . .

Would you like to be known as wise and discerning? Maybe you would like people to think of you as an interesting person and a good conversationalist.

The secret is to become a good listener. Effective listening is more than simply avoiding the bad habit of interrupting others while they are speaking or finishing their sentences. It is being content to listen to the entire thought of someone rather than waiting impatiently for your chance to respond. In this fast paced world, we have gotten out of the habit of really focusing on what the other person is saying and are already thinking ahead to our response before they're finished speaking. I've done that and probably you have too.

When we listen to people, really listen, we are saying to them that they are special and important to us. Besides, we learn more by listening than talking! People respond to this kindness in behavior. Therefore, they do feel special and they think that you are wonderful. Becoming a better listener will truly enhance our relationships. We'll become better wives, mothers, friends, etc. Others will think we are worth knowing. Listening will improve the quality of all our interactions and is the key to blessed relationships.

The quality of our relationship with our heavenly Father will also greatly improve if we strengthen our listening ears and wait upon Him. The blessings that come will have eternal value.

Read Proverbs 8:34-35 below:

*"Blessed is the man who listens to me, watching daily at my gates, waiting at the posts of my doors. For whoever finds me finds life, and obtains favor from the Lord."* NKJV

Our part of this promise is to _____.

God's promise is _____ and _____ to us.

I find myself spiritually listening more intently when things aren't going so well. Maybe that's because when things are beyond my control, I'm more focused on God. Is this statement true with you also? Any examples?

Listening to God is a habit we need to develop as God's women. He gave us each 2 ears and 1 mouth for a reason. Obviously, He wants us to use one more than the other!

One of the things that hinder us from hearing from the Lord is unconfessed sin. Here is what Psalms 66:18 has to say about that: *"If I regard iniquity in my heart, the Lord will not hear."* NKJV

If we are going to have an effective prayer life, sin has no place. Sin breaks down the communication between the believer and God. When we are really serious about wanting to hear God's voice, we will make every effort to keep our hearts pure.

Another reason we may not hear God's voice is that we really don't expect Him to actually speak to us. Maybe we think that we aren't worthy enough. God desires to speak to His children. Pray expecting and then wait on Him for an answer. He is a loving heavenly Father who wants us to listen for His voice. Look at John 10:27.

There are many ways in which God will speak to you. He may choose to speak to you: through His Word, through an audible voice or a feeling deep down in your being, or through dreams and visions, etc.

But probably the most common of all means is through the quiet inner voice. Isaiah 30:21 says, *"Your ears shall hear a word behind you, saying, This is the way, walk in it. Whenever you turn to the right hand or whenever you turn to the left."* NKJV

Sometimes we may be over anxious to hear His voice. Don't be so preoccupied that you miss hearing Him. Relax. It's been my experience that He often speaks when your mind is elsewhere. Or He will come to you in the middle of the night. What do you think the reason for that is? Yes, because you've been too busy to listen during the day! When do you sense God speaking to you most?

Another way God communicates with His children is through His Word. As you are reading and studying your Bible, keep your mind open for any lesson He might want you to learn. In a parable found in Matthew 13, Jesus says the Word that God shares is like seed thrown down by the farmer. It takes root in good soil, that is, the person who hears the word and understands it. However, if our minds are closed or on other things as we study, how can we hear any message God might have for us?

Have you noticed that your mind is the most active when your intentions are to study the Bible? You can think of things to put on your grocery list, remember that you had to make that important call and hundreds of other things when all you want to do is study your Bible for a few minutes. If you keep a pen and paper handy to write down these things to do later, you can keep your mind clear for the most important stuff!

Have you obeyed the last thing God told you to do? If you haven't, why would He tell you to do another thing? We can compare this to telling our children to do something over and over because they haven't listened the first time.

If we practice hearing God's voice, it becomes more of a habit. It's like picking up the phone and recognizing the voice of your friend . . . you know his voice because you've heard it so much. How blessed we are to have our Father God actually want to reveal Himself in such a personal and intimate way.

And speaking of the phone, when we are in need of guidance, the place to go first is to the throne not the phone. I know it seems easier, but remember the One who actually has the power to fix your problem is waiting to hear from you. It only makes sense that His voice is the one you seek above all others.

Another parable that seems to fit here is found in Matthew 7. It's the story of two builders. The man who built on solid rock represents everyone who hears and puts in practice God's guidance. The man who built on shifting sand symbolizes those who ignore God's truth and goes his own way. We know the lesson here. If we fail to act on the truth God reveals to us in any form He chooses, we are the ones who lose.

Your relationship with Him is the most important reason for wanting to hear the voice of God. True guidance is getting closer to the Guide. We grow to know the Lord better as He speaks to us and as we listen to Him and obey with a yielded heart. See 2 Peter 3:18 for more insight and a life goal.

We've probably all at one time or another followed some or all of these principles. But probably the hardest part of hearing God's voice is the waiting. But that too, can be rewarding. Just think of this. As you are waiting, you are totally focused on Him. And because of that focus, you'll receive little blessings along the way. And when you do receive the answer, how blessed you are in knowing that you were obedient.

*"Be still and know that I am God . . ." (Psalm 46:10)*NKJV

*"My soul, wait silently for God alone, for my expectation is from Him. He only is my rock and my salvation; He is my defense; I shall not be moved!"*(Psalm 62:5-6)NKJV

We are all called to pray and listen. Wait upon Him and listen. We have different spiritual gifts, but we're all called to pray and listen. We are in different stages of our spiritual journey and are involved in various ministries, but we are all called to pray and listen. Keep your heart and mind open to the leading of the Holy Spirit. Live life as God's women, not waiting for things to happen, make them happen. Remember, you are in partnership with your heavenly Father.

Be like the two fishermen who got trapped in a storm in the middle of the lake. One turned to the other and asked, "Should we pray, or should we row?" His wise companion responded, "Let's do both!" Wisdom says to bring God into the situation. Wisdom says to also respond with commonsense. Women of God need to learn to do both.

Blessings!

# 10

# ESTHER—WOMAN OF COURAGE

This story in which an orphaned, Jewish girl named Esther is the main character is an exciting one. It contains many elements of a best-selling novel or a #1 box office hit. There's drama, humor, a true villain, a beautiful heroine, several sub-plots all set in the beautiful surroundings of an exotic Persian palace. Besides all this, there is a surprise ending in which the "good guys" win!

In the first chapter of Esther, we read about a great feast in which the King is host to many of his men. There is much celebrating and drinking while the Queen was hostess in a separate banquet with the ladies. In verses 11-12 what happens to begin to make the way for God's plan for Esther and the Jewish people?

In verses 15-19 what was the consequence of Queen Vashti's actions?

In chapter two we learn that the King regrets his rash decision regarding Queen Vashti, but the decree cannot be reversed. So a search is made to find the most beautiful young woman in all the land. Our Esther is one of the young ladies. It sounds like the story of Cinderella doesn't it? But that was a fairy tale. Esther's story is not.

The King was hardly Prince Charming. In fact, he was a difficult, angry man who drank a lot. In contrast, Esther was pleasing, kind and a young woman of beauty both inside and out. As we read the book of Esther, we find her to be humble, wise and courageous. All of these virtues come into play as she is determined to act in the best interests of her people, the Jews.

We can learn from Esther about these three virtues: humility, courage and wisdom. But first let's talk a little about being prepared. Read chapter 2:12-14.

What preparations did the girls make before meeting the King?

We talk a lot about God's plan for our lives, but aren't there times when you feel that God isn't using you and isn't bringing forth any plan in your life at all? I believe those are the times God wants to prepare you for a future calling. We know that God doesn't waste any experiences you've had in life, but in the quiet, nothing happening times of life, we have the responsibility of learning all we can about Him. Trust in God to give you direction through the Holy Spirit's leading as to what you are to focus your study on. We know this preparation begins with prayer.

List some practical ways we can prepare for God to use us for future tasks.

1.

2.

3.

4.

During this very important preparation time there are several things to remember. We must stand firm in our faith and wait upon Him and we must keep our own counsel and listen intently for His voice. A wonderful, encouraging scripture to memorize is Jeremiah 29:11. Write it out here:


During this time of preparation, we see that Esther didn't demand her own way as she could have. Remember, she was in competition with a hundred or more girls, think American Idol or Survivor. But she remained unspoiled and humble. Read chapter 2:15-20.

Even after Esther was crowned queen, she was obedient to her uncle Mordecai.

How might have her life style in the royal palace and her position as queen changed her priorities and affected her actions?

Read Philippians 2:3-4

In what ways did Esther live out the truth of these verses?

As we look at these verses from a personal aspect, how can looking after other's interests before our own possibly benefit us?

The second virtue I want us to look at is courage. In the story of Ruth and in the story of Esther, we find a huge level of courage displayed. Does God only choose to use courageous people? NO! The saying goes—**GOD USES ORDINARY PEOPLE TO DO EXTRAORDINARY THINGS**. The EXTRA element in this is God!

The name of the Lord God is not mentioned once in the entire book of Esther, but He is seen in the actions of every development in this story of the God-fearing queen of the pagan king of Persia. When she learns of the plot to kill all the Jewish people, she did the only thing an ordinary person could do in a situation that was beyond her control. Read chapter 4:9-17.

How did she turn this crisis situation over to God?

The often quoted response from Mordecai in verse 14b is this: " . . . who *knows but that you've come to royal position for such a time as this?*" (NIV) Did this response convince Esther to approach the king?

What is significant about Mordecai's claim that if she remained completely silent at this time, relief and deliverance will arise for the Jews from another place? (See verse 14.)

What does Esther's decision to go before the king tell us about the quality of her character?

In a crisis situation, how do you typically respond? Do you (a) become hysterical; (b) become immobilized by fear; (c) pray; (d) swing into action; (e) try to escape; (f) react in some other way? Why do you think you respond this way?

God often puts His people in position without revealing His purpose. How could Esther have known when she was crowned Queen of Persia that she would save her people from extermination? How can any of us know for certain God's purpose for placing us in our particular circumstances? As I think about it, I feel the lesson here for us is to use the circumstances we find ourselves in to help or encourage people and to honor God whenever we can. (Even when we don't feel like it!)

The last virtue we'll talk about is wisdom. Jesus said that we're to be as gentle as doves, but as wise as serpents. Esther was both. In James 1:5 it says *"If any of you lack wisdom, he should ask God, who gives generously to all without finding fault and it will be given to him."* (NIV)

God knows that we will all face situations that require wisdom far beyond our own abilities. He supplied Esther with His wisdom in the tight places, just as He will do for us when we need it. Any of us, dear sister, has access to God's wisdom at any time, provided we know Him. Our part is to keep our minds open to His leading.

Read Esther 5:1-4

Why do you think that this was a wise approach?

What does the word intercession mean?

What giant requests to God do you consistently make on behalf of others?

A life principle we can take from Esther's story is this: Even though you are only one person, you can make a difference. You probably won't be called upon to help deliver a nation from extinction, but whatever your purpose is it will be a task that only you will be uniquely qualified to accomplish.

If you think God is not doing anything in your life right now, take a closer look. Maybe this time is your preparation time. Take this time of waiting to fill your heart and mind with the miraculous and amazing things of God.

Take advantage of every opportunity because you may find yourself in a position for such a time as this!

We've skipped over many parts of the book of Esther in the interest of time and space. I encourage you to read these ten chapters to fill in the blanks. It will be worth your time.

Blessings!

# 11

# I AM GOD'S WORKMANSHIP

I have friends who are "quilters". They make colorful, beautiful, unique masterpieces. Very fortunate is the person who receives one of these lovely pieces of art as a gift. Most quilters I know enjoy giving their handiwork away. I think it would be hard to imagine where to begin when you look at small piles of fabric of various colors, shapes and sizes. Or one big piece of fabric that you had to cut to be fitted and sewed together to make such beautiful treasures. It takes real craftsmanship to see the potential in the beginning and see it through to the lovely end result.

*"But now, O LORD, You are our Father; We are the clay, and You are the potter; and all we are the work of Your hand."* Isaiah 64:8 (NKJV)

What a beautiful thought that our Heavenly Father is taking us—lumps of clay that we are—and shaping us into a unique treasure to be used by Him. Our Father sees our potential by looking deep within us. With our permission, He will transform us into a beautiful and unique treasure for Himself.

The first step in this make-over process is to accept Jesus' gift of mercy and forgiveness of sin. But that's only the beginning. Great and wonderful things happen when we allow God to work in us. It's not an easy process. It's not a quick process either. In fact, it's a lifetime of transformation. But thanks be to the Father that He will never give up! That's a promise found in Philippians 1:6. Look it up and write it below:

It isn't always a pleasant experience, changes aren't always fun, but we are talking about a wonderful opportunity to be transformed into someone who God can use for His purposes here on planet Earth. We will be useful in working with Him to build His Kingdom. Partnering with God will bring to your life purpose and fulfillment, along with immeasurable joy and untold pleasure on this earth and Heavenly rewards in eternity.

We know that God loves us and He desires us to reach our full potential. This desire of His for each one of our lives will help us as we serve Him here on planet Earth. It will also go a long way:

in helping us to grow strong spiritually

our influence on others will have a larger impact

and the rewards of a fulfilling life will be greater.

All of this and much more because of a desire to become more like Jesus Christ. Is it possible to be holy in this life? The Word says to" *be holy for I am holy."* (1 Peter 1:16 NKJV) Some Christians seem content to only seek as much of God's grace as they think it takes to get to heaven, and no more. Such people are spiritually misguided, miserable or both.

However, many Christians want to be all that they can be in the Lord. They are willing to be molded and shaped by their Heavenly Father. They are interested in maximum Christianity that makes a practical difference in this life and beyond. These devoted Christ followers want nothing less than the best that God has for them and are willing to give nothing less than holy living requires. Are you that person?

What a shock to the system if we had to change the second we said "yes" to Christ! Thankfully, God in His graciousness has a different plan for us to grow more like His Son. The Word had a special insight into this in 2 Corinthians 3:18. Look at this verse and fill in the blanks below:

*"We are being changed from* _____ *to* _____*."* (NASB) In other words, God, through the Holy Spirit working in us, changes us a little at

a time. This enables us to constantly grow stronger and not give up wanting to be more like Jesus.

Some examples would be if one day you refused to listen to gossip or an off-colored joke. The next time you encountered these situations, it would be easier not take part and the next time, even easier. God working in you, making little changes daily. Or if someone around you was being grumpy and cranky, but you refused to let them rob you of your joy. When you choose victory over defeat, you are being transfigured into His very own image. You are gradually being freed from the bondage of the entanglements of this world and being made a vessel to be used by your Heavenly Father! How cool is that?!!

In 2 Corinthians 4, God calls us _____ of _____. Read verse 7 and fill in the blanks. This verse tells us that we possess a precious treasure—a power or light from God in our frail, human vessels that enables us to go beyond our own selves. Read in verses 8 and 9 to learn about what belonging to God can enable us to do.

All this comes from transforming knowledge through Jesus Christ, our Lord and Savior. Read verse 6 and write below.

Look at Isaiah 29:16.

_____ is the potter. _____ are the clay.

Are you dissatisfied with the way God made you?

How would you like to be different?

Think of your spiritual gifts. How can you develop them for greater use for God?

Although God could instantly transform us, He has chosen to mold and shape us slowly. Just as He allowed the Israelites to take over the Promised Land *"little by little"* (Deut 7:22) so they wouldn't be overwhelmed, He is changing us slowly into the likeness of His Son, Jesus Christ. It's for our own benefit really, because we are all slow learners and even when we think we've learn our lesson, we end up doing the same dumb thing over and over again!

There was a popular button years ago with the letters PBPGINFWMY. It stands for "Please Be Patient, God Is Not Finished With Me Yet." Thankfully, dear sisters, He's not finished with us either, so let's keep on moving and learning and encouraging each other 'til Jesus returns.

Blessings!

# 12

# GOD'S WORD—DIGGING DEEPER

*²² "But be doers of the word, and not hearers only, deceiving yourselves. ²³ For if anyone is a hearer of the word and not a doer, he is like a man observing his natural face in a mirror; ²⁴ for he observes himself, goes away, and immediately forgets what kind of man he was. ²⁵ But he who looks into the perfect law of liberty and continues in it, and is not a forgetful hearer but a doer of the work, this one will be blessed in what he does."* James 1:22-25 NKJV

There are people who sit in church and listen to the same sermon you do but don't seem to change. Many people read their Bible, but they don't apply it in their everyday life, so nothing changes. It seems like they sit back and think that just because they have heard and read the Word, it should bring change into their life. But change doesn't happen automatically; a person has to be a doer of the Word, not a hearer only.

Which one are you—a hearer or a doer?

Have you seen changes in your spiritual life in the last year?

How about the last six months?

Look up the following verses and in your own words, state what God wants us to do about His Word.

Deuteronomy 11:18a—

Proverbs 7:3b—

In Matthew 4:4, 7, 10

How did Jesus overcome Satan's temptations?

Do you see how you might apply this example when you are facing trials?

In Colossians 3:16, are the words: *"Let the Word of Christ dwell in you richly"* (NKJV) what do you think that means?

There are many benefits of studying God's Word and knowing where your favorite verses are found. Psalm 119:11 states that *"Your Word have I hidden in my heart, that I might not sin against You."* (NKJV) Memorizing scripture verses and passages is a good way to *"hide God's Word in your heart."* Blessings of wisdom, strength, comfort, etc. will come during life situations if you first commit scripture to memory.

I heard somewhere that after 24 hours you may accurately remember:

> 5% of what you hear,
> 15% of what you read,
> 35% of what you study,
> 57% of what you see and hear
> But you can remember 100% of what you memorize!

Here's the bad news—I also read somewhere that we are at the peak of our memorizing skills when we are in the sixth grade. So, even though we have to work a little harder, memorizing the scripture is well worth the effort!

Look at Psalms 119:105.

Why do you think God's Word is described as a lamp and a light?

Other light from the Word:

Look up these verses and define in your own words what God says about **wisdom.**

Proverbs 3:7

James 3:17

James 1:5-6

What do these verses have to say about **worry**?

Matthew 6:25-27

What do these verses say about the **protection** God will provide?

Deuteronomy 31:8

Deuteronomy 33:12, 11

Chronicles 16:9a

What about the **strength** He provides?

Philippians 4:13

God gives comfort to us in times of need. There are many verses, especially in the Psalms that speak of comfort. But in 2 Corinthians 1:3-5 what does He command us to do with the **comfort** He gives us?

Share a time when you have been on the giving end of comfort.

Share a time when you're been on the receiving end of comfort.

God works through His people to bring comfort and encouragement to those in need. As we go through this journey, dear sisters, we will experience both the giving and the receiving of comfort.

Here are some helpful tips as you study God's word:

1. Develop a passion for God's word. It is so unlike any other book. It is able to change lives. There are only two things on planet Earth that are eternal: people and God's word.
2. Don't limit your knowledge to second-hand information. Read and study for yourself.
3. Don't skip over a word or phase you're not familiar with—look it up in a commentary, Bible dictionary or another Bible translation. Doing so will make you remember it more.

4. When reading about a character or an account, put yourself in that place—how can this apply to my life?
5. Create a list of favorite verses—read them often—memorize them.
6. Read the Bible every day, because after all, people have died to bring it to you.
7. Pray that the Holy Spirit will teach you things as you read and study the word.

It is God's desire for us to be life-time learners of His Word. I heard someone say one time that she already read the Bible through once and saw no need to read it again. Well that sister sure missed the point!

There are always new and wonderful things to learn as we seek out and study the principles, promises, and characters of the Bible. How can we claim a promise if we don't know what He has promised? How are we going to know what God expects of us if we don't read His commands? The knowledge of His principles will lead you in a smoother, richer spiritual journey.

Pray before you open your Bible that the Holy Spirit will teach you those things to bring blessings and benefits to your life. If we are sincere in our prayer, we can be assured that it is one prayer He is eager to answer! The more we know and apply to our lives, the closer relationship we can enjoy with our Heavenly Father.

In 2 Peter 3:18 we read, *"but grow in the grace and knowledge of our Lord and Savior Jesus Christ. To Him be the glory both now and forever. Amen"* (NKJV)

Blessings!

# 13

# DID YOU DO THIS FOR ME?

*"Knowing that you were not redeemed with corruptible things, like silver or gold, from your aimless conduct received by tradition from your fathers, but with the precious blood of Christ, as of a lamb without blemish and without spot. He indeed was foreordained before the foundation of the world, but was manifest in these last times for you."* 1 Peter1:18-20 NKJV

As we approach Easter this year, let's pause and ponder (Selah) and try to understand the limitless depth of God's love for us. Let us not let another year go by without trying to feel the intensity of the sacrifice Jesus made for us six hours one Friday.

THE DIADEM OF PAIN
WHICH SLICED YOUR GENTLE FACE,
THREE SPIKES PIERCING FLESH AND WOOD TO HOLD YOU IN
YOUR PLACE.
THE NEED FOR BLOOD I UNDERSTAND.
YOUR SACRIFICE I EMBRACE.
BUT THE BITTER SPONGE, THE CUTTING SPEAR,
THE SPIT UPON YOUR FACE?
DID IT HAVE TO BE A CROSS?
DID NOT A KINDER DEATH EXIST

THAN SIX HOURS HANGING BETWEEN LIFE AND DEATH,
ALL SPURRED BY A BETRAYER'S KISS?
"OH FATHER," YOU POSE,
HEART-STILLED AT WHAT COULD BE,
"IM SORRY TO ASK, BUT I LONG TO KNOW,
DID YOU DO THIS FOR ME?"
Author unknown

## A WEEK IN THE LIFE OF JESUS

SUNDAY:

Jesus and His disciples came to the town of _____ (Mark 11:1 NIV) He sent 2 of His disciples before them to find a _____.(verse 2) When they returned from their errand, Jesus mounted the colt and they made their way into the city, an event known as the _____ _____.(verses 8-10) On this day, all of those following Christ must have been elated. Kings rode horses into battle but rode donkeys at times of peace. The way the crowd responded to Jesus' entrance that day was the response they would give to royalty. No wonder the Pharisees were nervous and wanted Jesus out of the way. In fact, in Luke 19:39, they asked Jesus to _____ His disciples. And Jesus answered them by saying that if they are silent then, *"the* _____ *will cry out!"* (verse 40)

In verse 41, we see that as Jesus approached the city, He _____. He knew that as joyful and welcoming as the crowd was, that they would soon reject Him. He is grieved when we reject Him also. The human heart is fickle. As devoted Christ followers, we must always guard our hearts.

MONDAY:

In Matthew 21:12-14, Jesus _____ the moneychangers out of the _____ and healed a _____ man. In the first situation, Jesus had righteous anger. We too, need to not be passive and work to change things that are not up to God's standards, according to His word. In the second situation, Jesus gives us an example of compassion. When we see a need that we can do something about, it is our privilege to fill it. We are blessed to be a blessing!

## TUESDAY:

Read Mark 12:14-17. The religious leaders try to trap Jesus. They really didn't know who they were dealing with! The world tries to trip us up in many ways. Challenges come in many forms and at unexpected times. That is why we must always be prepared to answer those challenges with the truth from God's Word. Use God's Word as the standard of truth in your life. The way to be prepared with the truth is to know what's in His Word and to be willing to share it as you have the opportunity. The world desperately needs to hear that Jesus hung on the cross for them too.

## WEDNESDAY:

As the chief priests and the scribes were plotting to kill Jesus, He attended a dinner party. Let's read about it in Mark 14:3-9. The dinner was held at the home of _____ the _____. What totally unpredictable thing happened while the dinner party was going on?

Although several of the disciples disagreed with this action, saying it was not practical and a waste of money, Jesus had a different opinion found in verse 9.

I believe it was a celebration of love on the part of this woman. It's a good example of the quality of love you can have in your personal relationship with God. C.S. Lewis wrote . . . **"A man's spiritual health is exactly proportional to his love for God."** If we are to enjoy the spiritual health that God intends for our lives, we must praise Him and love Him as we focus on Him only. Never be concerned that you are worshipping Him too much.

## THURSDAY:

This day was the first of eight days known as Passover, the celebration that commemorates the protection God gave to His people when they were slaves in Egypt. They were to put lamb's blood on their doorposts, so the death angel would pass over their house and in doing this, the first born of their households would be saved from death.

Jesus and His disciples celebrated together what has come to be known as the Last Supper. In an incredible display of love and servant hood, Jesus knelt down and washed the feet of His friends, giving them an example of the kind of behavior He expected of them. It's amazing to think that although Jesus knew what was going to happen to Him in just a few short hours, He wanted to do this for His friends. Even more amazing to me is the fact that He washed the feet of the one He knew would betray Him. How does this act of humility and love make you feel?

During the meal, Jesus instituted the practice we now call Communion. Read Jesus' words in Mark: 22-25. The bread represents Jesus' _____. The wine (or juice) represents Jesus' _____. When we receive communion, we are to remember Jesus' shed blood and broken body and the covenant we have with God because He gave His Son to stand in our place. Jesus' six hours on the cross can't be made an empty ritual, but a meaningful time of forgiveness and strengthening of our faith.

THURSDAY EVENING AND FRIDAY

In Mark 14:32 we read that Jesus and the disciples walked to the G_____ of G_____. Why did Jesus go there? _____ In verse 36, He prayed. "Not_____ will, but _____. Jesus didn't want to die. He wished for a less painful way to carry out this task, but He submitted to His Father's will.

## GOD'S WILL, NOTHING MORE, NOTHING LESS, NOTHING ELSE

An excellent lesson for us to remember is found in verse 38. What is it? _____ _____

That night led to Jesus' arrest and His eventual death on the cross. It started with a betrayer's kiss and the abandonment of all His close friends. We've all read the account of that long night . . . Jesus standing before the Sanhedrin, Peter's denial of Jesus, Pilate, the beatings and the crown of thorns and Jesus great lesson in forgiveness as He hung on the cross.

I don't know about you, but I don't want to go to any more passion plays. However, it is good for us to be reminded of these events, because until we feel our responsibility in Jesus' death, we will not understand the extent of our sin nature or the depth of Christ's forgiveness. We deserve to be the ones punished for our sin. Instead, Jesus, the sinless one, volunteered to take the punishment in our place.

# AM I MY SISTER'S KEEPER?

I think you'll agree that it's been a long winter. I do like to see the first snowfall like we get here in Michigan, but my real favorite would be the last snowfall and the first sign of spring. I've noticed that the first few warm days of spring puts a smile on most everyone's face.

Spring is about hope. Especially here in the north, we are excited to see the first green blades of grass and all the other new life of nature as it is resurrected into an explosion of beauty. How wonderful and loving our Heavenly Father was to plan for the resurrection of His Son in the springtime of the year! The resurrection of Jesus brought us the assurance that He has the power over death. In Him, there is eternal life for the Christian.

When the women went to the tomb on that first Easter morning, they were told *"He is risen, He is not here."* (Luke 24:6) This was unexpected and shocking news to them. Their mission that morning was to prepare their friend's body for the grave, but instead, they saw that the large stone that sealed the entrance of the tomb was rolled away. Don't you think that there was a glimmer of hope in the back of their minds? Verse 8 says that *"they remembered His words,"* that He would be raised up on the third day.

As you approach Easter week, pause and ponder (Selah) the story as if you've never heard it before. Or ponder it as if you've heard it 5,000 times—and it's just beginning to sink in.

This year on Good Friday, sometime between 9:00am and 3:00pm (the six hours Jesus hung on the cross) don't forget to thank Him for paying the debt you owed to be reconciled with God. And on Resurrection Sunday whisper the question that was asked in the beginning of the lesson . . . "Did you do this for me?" You know the answer.

The last days of Jesus' life is found in all four gospels. Read these accounts for a better understanding of Jesus purpose here on planet Earth.

Matthew 21 to the end of the book.

Mark 11 to the end of the book.

Luke 19:28 to the end of the book.

John 12 to the end of the book.

Blessings!

# 14

# ROCK ON

## Jesus is my Rock

*"The Lord is my rock and my fortress and my deliverer, my God, my ROCK in whom I take refuge."* 2 Samuel 22:2 NIV

These are the words David sang to God after He delivered him from the hands of King Saul. Aren't you glad that these words were recorded for our inspiritation and as a great source of strength for us?

These words and many others in the Bible refer to God as being a rock, or a fortress, or a shelter. Many of these references are in the Psalms written by David. Much of David's early life was spent running from enemies who were literally trying to take his life. Hopefully we'll never find ourselves in that situation, but can't we all relate to David a little bit?

But we certainly do have an enemy chasing us—it is the enemy of our souls. Sometimes the enemy comes in the form of discouragement, or discontentment, or depression, or jealousy, or distrust, or resentment—you get the idea. Now when the enemy is hot on our trail, closing in for the kill and we find ourselves out of breath, we can call on the name of the Lord, because of a wonderful promise in Proverbs 18:10. Look it up and fill in the blanks.

*"The _____ of the Lord is a _____ _____; the righteous runs into it and is _____." NIV*

In practical terms, what is this verse telling us to do? _____ And what is God's part in this promise? _____

I appreciate the fact that I have this wonderful source of strength and security. When I feel weak, He gives me strength. When I am afraid, He assures me that He will take care of me. And to plug into this Source, I merely have to call on His name in faith.

A hymn we sometimes sing is:

**"Oh Jesus is a rock in a weary land, a weary land, a weary land . . . a shelter in the time of storm."**

We all get weary now and then. Sometimes it's because of busyness, or our physical health or even our spiritual health has us discouraged. Sometimes we get no support from our loved ones and feel unappreciated. Sometimes people disappoint us. Many things in this earthy life can make us weary. The cure for weariness is to go to God and His Word for a good dose of out of this world encouragement. Look at Psalm 31:1-5.

This is another psalm written by David. He was weary and tired of running from those who wanted to kill him and in the midst of this misery, he still knew where to turn. What do you do first in your crisis situations?

Another lovely, old hymn goes like this:

**"On Christ the solid Rock I stand, all other ground is sinking sand . . ."**

Jesus taught a parable (an earthly story with a heavenly meaning) in Matthew 7:24-27. Let's look at it together.

What does building your house on a rock represent?

What do the rain and the wind symbolize?

What happens if your house is built on sand?

What is the heavenly meaning of this earthly story?

When we put our trust in Jesus, the Rock, we are standing on solid ground and will never sink as long as we keep our eyes on Him!

Jesus tells another parable in Luke 8:5-8 about a farmer planting seeds. Look at it please.

Jesus explains the meaning of this parable in verses 11-15.

Seeing Jesus as our Rock is a good thing. Having a hard, rocky heart—not good. Many people try to get to heaven by "being good" and by "doing good". This is wrong thinking. No one enters heaven just by being good and doing good works. The great Rock is Jesus. The only way to the Father and eternity in heaven with Him is through faith in Jesus Christ. For the "be-good, do-good" people, He is a stumbling block. For people whose faith is in Him, He is a stepping stone.

Some friends and I had a discussion a while ago about calling Jesus a Rock. One person didn't like that name, because although a rock is one of the most solid and strong elements in nature, it can be broken into many pieces. Well, after I thought about that a while, it came to me that if Jesus is our Rock, we can be the stones that are broken off Him. Do you agree or disagree? Explain.

1 Peter 2:4 speaks of us as living stones and that we are chosen and precious in God's sight. Peter goes on to explain that we believers as living stones are used in building the church with Jesus as the Cornerstone. Also see Ephesians 2:20-21.

Have you ever wondered, "What is my purpose on the earth?" Well I'll tell you—to be living stones used to build God's church. In practical terms what does that look like? Well here are a few things that I thought of:

Through our words and actions allow the salvation we've accepted through Jesus, the Rock, to reach others so they can know salvation too.

Look for opportunities to share the good news about Jesus Christ and what He's done in our own lives.

We can be God's hands and feet on the planet Earth just by looking for ways to be kind and helpful. Doing this can lead to spiritual matters.

Simply put—we are to:
Wash what is dirty
Water what is dry
Heal what is wounded
Warm what is cold
Guide what goes off the road
Love those who are least lovable, because they need it most.

Romans 15:1-6 says it in a better and more spiritual way. Look at it please.
This passage says—we are to:
Carry other's burdens
Be pleasing to others in Jesus' name
Build up and encourage others in their faith
Have patience with all unbelievers and also your sisters and brothers in the faith
So that one day we'll all with one voice, sing praises to our Lord and Savior and Rock, Jesus Christ!

Spring always reminds us of Easter and the work Jesus did for us six hours one Friday. The awesome thing about Easter was the huge stone that was rolled away from the tomb. It showed us two things:

1. That the tomb was empty and . . .
2. It symbolized Jesus' mighty strength and power—especially when we consider that Jesus didn't need for the stone to be rolled away to get out. The stone was rolled away for our benefit so we would know that the work Jesus came to do on planet Earth was finished—until He returns for us.

Spring is a special time for me. It is the time I celebrate my spiritual birthday. I've been a new creation in Christ for 30+ years. There have been many opportunities during those years to claim God's strength through His Son, Jesus Christ. God has proven to me over and over again how faithful and loving He is. And when I need a solid Rock to stand on, He is there for me.

The Bible can mean many things to us. One thing it should always be for us is personal. The following scripture is another psalm inspired by the Holy

Spirit and written by David. Let's read it together, out loud and as we read, fill in each blank with your name.

"_____ soul finds rest in God alone; _____ salvation comes from Him. He alone is _____ Rock and _____ salvation; He is _____ fortress, _____ will never be shaken." Psalm 62:1-2 NIV

**"Jesus is my Rock and my name is on the Roll!"**

Blessings!

# 15

# FRIENDSHIP—ICING ON THE CAKE

I make a wonderful white cake. It is an old-fashioned vanilla cake recipe that I got from my Mother. Sometimes I put a peanut butter frosting on it and it is rich, sweet, and yummy! That is what I think friendship is in the "cake of life"—rich, sweet, and yummy! Oh yes. Friendship is one of the sweetest gifts God gives us to enjoy in this lifetime. It is a great encouragement to have friends in the trials of this life also.

Have you found this to be true? That in the trials of life, friends can do what you sometimes are unable to do? Pray for instance or see things objectively when you are too close to the situation, etc. Share your thoughts.

There are many qualities that describe what a friend is or does. Take a look at the following list and put a **check** in front of 10 of the most important attributes to you. After you've checked those off, **circle** 5 qualities that you possess as a friend.

Are there any qualities that you think you need to work on? **Underline** those.

(A)ccepts you as you are
(B)elieves in "you"
(C)alls you just to say "HI"

(D)oesn't give up on you!
(E)nvisions the whole of you (even the unfinished part)
(F)orgives your mistakes
(G)ives unconditionally
(H)elps you
(I)nvites you over
(J)ust "be" with you
(K)eeps you close at heart
(L)oves you for who you are
(M)akes a difference in your life
(N)ever judges
(O)ffers support
(P)icks you up
(Q)uiets your fears
(R)aises your spirits
(S)ays nice things about you
(T)ells you the truth when you need to hear it
(U)nderstands you
(V)alues you
(W)alks beside you
(X)-plains things you don't understand
(Y)ells when you won't listen and
(Z)aps you back to reality

(author unknown ... e-mail)

Friendships are vital to your relationship with God. Your friends are either pulling you down (away from God) or pulling you along and/or up (toward God). And you are doing the same for them. What do these scriptures have to say about the company you are to keep?

1 Corinthians 15:33

Proverbs 22:24-25

This is not to say that we shouldn't have friends who are non-believers. Of course we should. We are to walk before them as an example of who Christ is. And we must pray for them to come to a saving knowledge of Jesus in their own lives. (Then they are <u>forever friends!</u>) We must also pray for our

Christian friends. We all need prayer support as we live and work in this world that is not our home.

Let's look at some verses in Proverbs to understand the insights that Solomon gives us in the area of relationships.

Proverbs 18:24
Proverbs 14:20
Proverbs 19:4

From the following Proverbs, describe the qualities Solomon considers to be important in good friends.

Proverbs 11:13
Proverbs 17:9
Proverbs 17:17
Proverbs 20:3
Proverbs 22:11
Proverbs 27:9

Moses, Abraham and David are described in the Bible as friends of God. What qualities would you have to have in order to be a good friend of God? Discuss and write your ideas here:

What a blessing it is to have friends! You've heard the saying, "to have friends, you must first be one"? Make your mind up to be a trustworthy, encouraging and loyal friend. Sow the seed of friendship today. Treasure the people in your life who are your loyal and true friends. Friends are a wonderful gift from God.

**A true friend is someone who reaches for your hand and touches your heart.**

## STARLIGHT CAKE
(My Mom's vanilla cake recipe)

| **Large cake** | **Small cake** |
|---|---|
| Flour 2 ½ cups | 1 ½ cups |
| Sugar 1 ½ cups | 1 cup |
| Baking powder 3 teaspoons | 2 teaspoons |

| | |
|---|---|
| Shortening-(soft) 1/3 cup | 3 ½ tablespoons |
| Milk 1 cup | 2/3 cup |
| Vanilla 1 ½ teaspoons | 1 teaspoon |
| Eggs 2 | 1 egg |

Use a 13x9 or a 8x8 pan, lightly grease. Bake @ 350 for 20-30 minutes, depending on the size of the pan and your oven. Don't over bake. Cool, add frosting or not. Enjoy.

Blessings!

# 16

# WOMEN OF INFLUENCE

Matthew 5:13-16:

*"Let me tell you why you are here. You're here to be salt-seasoning that brings out the God-flavors of this earth. If you lose your saltiness, how will people taste Godliness? You've lost your usefulness and will end up in the garbage.*

*Here's another way to put it: You're here to be light, bringing out the God-colors in the world. God is not a secret to be kept. We're going public with this, as public as a city on a hill... Shine! Keep open house; be generous with your lives. By opening up to others, you'll prompt people to open up with God, this generous Father in heaven."* THE MESSAGE

One thing we see in this passage is that to be an influence for God, we must be around people. Answer these questions about yourself:

Am I too busy for girlfriend time?
Have I drifted away from relationships such as Sunday school class or small group Bible studies or prayer groups?
What can I do to create deeper friendships in my life?
Do I look for ways to encourage others as I walk through my daily life?

wonderful New Testament example of that last question found in 2. Read the story of Dorcas in these verses.

How was Dorcas described in verse 36?

In verses 37-38 we see that Dorcas took sick and died. Her friends tended to her body, as we might expect. Why do you think they thought it was important to send for Peter?

What did Peter find upon his arrival in Joppa? (verse 39)

In verses 40-41, God did a miracle through Peter and brought Dorcas back to life!

How wonderful and merciful He is! Describe your feelings when you hear of God's mighty works such as this.

Read verse 42, and summarize the amazing conclusion of this story.

I read this saying the other day and it seems to fit here . . .

**WHEN YOU WERE BORN, YOU WERE CRYING WHILE THOSE STANDING AROUND YOU WERE SMILING. WHEN YOU DIE, MAY YOU BE SMILING WHILE THOSE STANDING AROUND YOU ARE CRYING.** Author unknown

It tells us in the story of Dorcas that she made many articles of clothing for people. Do you think as she was passing out these garments, she was sprinkling around the salt too?

In biblical times, salt served three main functions: it purified, preserved, and added flavor. How can we as Christ followers, perform each of these functions in our culture today?

Purifying—

Preserving—

Flavoring—

Describe a time when you've seen someone act as salt in a specific situation.

Read Colossians 4:5-6. What do you think Paul means by conversations that is "seasoned with salt"? (remember the 3 functions of salt)

## "CHRISTIANS WHO ARE WORTH THEIR SALT, WILL MAKE OTHERS THIRSTY."

Let's make this personal. If we are salty Christians, shouldn't we be thirsty as well? Matthew 5:6 says that *"we are blessed if we hunger and thirst after righteousness."* (NKJV) What does that verse mean to you?

Can we make others thirsty if we aren't thirsty ourselves?

Look at Psalm 42:1-2

If we are serious about our faith and want to grow spiritually, we must be constantly seeking knowledge from the Bible and through spending time with the Lord. Our pursuit of His presence will be obvious to others and our influence will be felt as a *"sweet fragrance of Christ."* (2 Corinthians 2:15 AMP)

Let's look again at Matthew 5:14-16.

In these verses, Jesus calls us *"the light of the world"*. (NKJV) According to this passage, when are we most effective as light?

When are we least effective?

What are some keys to being "shiny" Christians?

Psalm 34:5
Daniel 12:3
2 Corinthians 3:18
Philippians 2:14-16

As women, I believe that God put us in the role of natural influencers. We are daughters, sisters, wives, mothers, and friends. We teach our children. We are an example to others. As God's women, we need to be sure that our influence is of eternal value. Our purpose here on planet earth is to teach, train, encourage, and lead those under our influence into the Kingdom of Heaven. A pretty heavy responsibility, I'd say. How can we be sure that we are influencing in the right way? How can we be sure that the world doesn't influence us instead of the other way around?

Look at Romans 12:1-2

What does scripture warn against here?

What is the alternative to conformity to the world?

We as Christians need to be in the world, but not a part of it. If the world is in us—God can't use us. We can't be a reflection of His light. A boat is made to be in the water, but there's a big problem when water gets in the boat.

I John 4:4—" . . . *greater is He that is in you, than he that is in the world.*" (NASB)

Use the tools of the world to win hearts for Jesus, but never compromise the Word of God. The Bible is the standard of truth. Romans 1:16 says, " . . . *I am not ashamed of the gospel, because it is the power of God for the salvation of everyone who believes . . .*"(NKJV)

To be an influence in our world with eternal value is to be Christ-like in all areas of our lives. Our influence is to be a stepping stone, not a stumbling block . . . . eternity hangs in the balance.

Blessings!

# 17

# THE 4:13's—THE GIFTS OF JESUS

One of my first favorite verses is Philippians 4:13 which states: *"I can do all things through Christ, who strengthens me."* (NKJV) At the time, I was teaching CYC (that's a Wednesday night kid's class in the old days) to sixth graders. I was a fairly new Christian back then and I thought I *really* could do all things . . . you know how newbies are!

I've learned since then that the gift of strength and power comes from the gifts Jesus gives those whose life is committed to Him. I also learned that when we partner with Jesus, the possibilities are endless!

Our study today is about five gifts given to believers by Jesus that are found in the scripture reference 4:13. Here are the five:

John 4:13 . . . satisfaction
Acts 4:13 . . . transformation
Ephesians 4:13 . . . inspiration
Philippians 4:13 . . . power
1 Thessalonians 4:13-14 . . . comfort

John 4:13 . . . *"Jesus answered and said to her, "Whoever drinks of this water will thirst again,"* (NKJV)

This verse comes from the passage where Jesus was talking to the woman at the well. Let's read the whole story starting with John 4:3 through 14.

Have you ever been so thirsty that nothing will satisfy your thirst but a nice big, cold glass of water? Of course, as we already know, Jesus was talking about more than water. Jesus knew all about this woman and the life she was living. He knew about her weaknesses and past sins and He also knew about her potential and the plans He had for her. He knew what would bring satisfaction and fulfillment to her life. This was not a chance encounter.

None of us have ever had a "chance encounter" with God. That's not the way He operates. He desires a relationship with each one of us. When we say "yes" to His Son, Jesus, He throws a party in heaven! Name some things that are different in your life today since you've tasted the *"living water"*.

King David was gifted to put together wonderful words and phases that came from his heart and speaks to our hearts today. He wrote a beautiful passage about his satisfaction in God in Psalm 63:1-8. Read it and share your thoughts.

David may have written this psalm when he was running from King Saul. It sounds like he was troubled and lonely. Those are the times when we earnestly seek the Lord. Let's not be ones who will seek His hand and not His face. Dear sisters, Father God wants us to share from the heart at all times. The good news is that through Jesus there are resources to satisfy needs at every level of human life.

Acts 4:13 *"Now when they saw the boldness of Peter and John, and perceived that they were uneducated and untrained men, they marveled. And they realized that they had been with Jesus."* (NKJV)

Read Acts 4:1 through 13 to understand the whole story.

What you do think it was that changed these men from simple folks to amazing messengers sent to bring God's good news?

Being uneducated and untrained is not enough of an excuse to not be a bold witness for the cause of the Kingdom of God. God has given us powerful resources to tell others about Him. The Holy Spirit is ready and able to work through a person whose heart is willing. Have you ever had the experience of being bold and later wondered where "that" came from? Share if you will.

We are responsible for our training. We learn through the Word of God, daily prayer and through our past experiences in life. When God has taught you a life lesson, write it down. (a daily journal is a good thing) He doesn't waste anything. Our life experiences can be an encouragement to others. Writing them in a journal helps us to remember.

If we aren't willing to be teachable, we'll never reach God's full potential for our lives. How has the Holy Spirit working within you transformed you? Any examples?

Ephesians 4:13 ..."*[That it might develop] until we all attain oneness in the faith and in the comprehension of the [full and accurate] knowledge of the Son of God, that [we might arrive] at really mature manhood (the completeness of personality which is nothing less than the standard height of Christ's own perfection), the measure of the stature of the fullness of the Christ and the completeness found in Him.*" AMP

The beginning of this passage talks about the importance of unity in the body of Christ—how we all need to work together for the benefit of all and for the glory of the Lord. If we are at odds with each other and fight against one another, how can we accomplish anything positive? And how would our Christian witness be to those we want to bring into the kingdom?

We can work together effectively because God gave us all different spiritual gifts and talents and beyond that He gave us love as a fruit of the Spirit so our spiritual gifts would blend together as one complete body. It is our responsibility to define our particular gifts and develop them for the good of us personally and the rest of the body. When we enthusiastically do this we are glorifying God and fulfilling the purpose of the spiritual gifts.

For a period of about three years, God call my husband John and I to be part of a core group starting a church plant in a city about thirty miles from our small town. Let me tell you that we were pretty comfortable serving in our own church with our own church family right in our own town. However, God had different plans for us at that time and so we served faithfully and willing until He called us to come back to our home church.

One of the important elements of that church plant was the fact that all seventeen members of the core group had different gifts. Some of us were musically gifted; others had the gift of hospitality and made excellent greeters. One had financial skills and so she became the treasurer. Some were gifted teachers of the Word and all of us became gifted in setting up and taking down chairs, tables, music equipment and such. And of course, we had Pastor Dale, our wonderful pastor. We each had an opportunity to share our unique gifts to make the whole thing possible and God was glorified because His purposes were served.

Philippians 4:13 . . ."*I can do all things through Christ who strengthens me.*" NKJV

Sometime in our life we have tried to be super-mom or super-woman by our own strength and power. How has this worked out for you? Good news, sisters, we don't have to do things under our own steam! That's one of the glorious changes God makes when the Holy Spirit is in residence. We are able to rely on His strength and power. Enough of this self-sufficiency! We don't need to prove anything to anyone. Our identity is found in the One who created us. He has created us with the freedom of choice, but He desires that we choose dependence and trust in Him.

We find many expressions of faith and trust in the Bible such as this one: *"Surely God is my salvation; I will trust and not be afraid. The Lord, is my strength and my song; he has become my salvation."* Isaiah 12:2 (NIV) The prophet Isaiah also writes, *"He gives strength to the weary,"* and *"those who hope in the Lord will renew their strength,"* (see Isaiah 40:29,31)

When we concentrate on what the scripture says about the glorious, all-powerful God living in our lives, we feel changed into a more capable being. Think about this; God's presence gives strength when we are weary, so much so that we feel like singing! Our hope and strength come from Him to all those who ask. And finally nothing that comes into my life is greater than God's power to overcome.

Here's a question for you . . . do you worry? Do you think God worries? If we worry and God doesn't worry then our thoughts are not matching His. If the words we speak tend to be negative and not positive then our words are not lining up with His words. The power and strength and authority we have in our lives come from being in God's presence. We can do all things only <u>through Him!</u>

1 Thessalonians 4:13-14 ... *"Now also we would not have you ignorant, brethren, about those who fall asleep [in death], that you may not grieve [for them] as the rest do who have no hope [beyond the grave]. ¹⁴For since we believe that Jesus died and rose again, even so God will also bring with Him through Jesus those who have fallen asleep [in death]."* AMP

The church at Thessalonica was a young church of new believers who were full of faith but had questions. Paul wrote this letter to answer those questions. Doesn't it seem like when we are new believers, we are full of enthusiasm but there is still so much we don't know or understand? One thing they wanted to know was: what would happen to believers who died before Christ returned? Wouldn't they miss out on this wonderful event?

In Thessalonians 4:13-18, Paul answers this question. Let's read it together.

What happens to the believers who died before Christ returns?

What happens to believers who are still alive at His Second Coming?

What are your thoughts on the Second Coming of Christ? Does thinking about it make you anxious or excited? Does this passage answer any questions you might have?

In 1 Thessalonians 4:17 are Paul's words ... *"And so shall we ever be with the Lord."* (NASB) This is the basic hope of all believers of Jesus. It is this truth that brings comfort to those of us who look for His return. More than any other message in all of the scriptures, comfort of the saints is derived from the promise of Christ's return. We can withstand all kinds of circumstances when we have this hope.

In these few verses from the 4:13's we've talked about some of the gifts that are available to us through Jesus that will enrich and enhance our lives here on planet Earth.

~ The gift of satisfaction is a resource that will bring fulfillment and contentment in many areas of our daily lives.

~ The gift of transformation brings positive changes in our lives that makes us more like Jesus and brings us to a closer relationship with the Father.

~ The gift of inspiration enables us to attain oneness within our church family and completeness in our own spiritual walk.

~ The gift of power gives us the strength, power and authority to do all things through Christ.

~ The gift of comfort comes from the assurance of an eternal future with God in heaven.

I pray for all of us to tear open these gifts with great excitement and enthusiasm and use them fully as we wait expectantly for Jesus return!

Blessings!

# 18

# PRAYER—IT IS A PRIVILEGE

Two things that we as Christians sometimes do that really bother me—

1. We sometimes say "well I've done everything I can think of, all I can do now is pray—"
2. When called to pray in a public setting, we sometimes have an attitude of "why pick on me"?

PRAYER IS A PRIVILEGE! Things happen when God's people pray. Why wouldn't we jump at the chance at being a part of that?

1 Peter 3:12a states—

*"For the eyes of the Lord are upon the righteous (those who are upright and in right standing with God), and His ears are attentive to their prayer."* (AMP)

Just think—the ears of the Creator of the world—the One who can do anything—are open to our prayers. What a privilege we have to be able to communicate with Him through prayer. Just one of the many blessings we have as God's children!

When you pray, picture yourself in the throne room of God Almighty, the God of the universe, Creator of all. Picture yourself there, because that is where you are when you pray. How should you approach God's throne? Look at Hebrews 4:14-16.

According to these verses in Hebrews, who intercedes for us?

Discuss the difference between boldness and arrogance.

Here are some reasons that we pray. Look at the scriptures (taken from the NIV) and fill in the blanks.

~It is God's _____ that we do so. 1 Thessalonians 5:18

~Prayer is the example of _____. Hebrews 5:7

~Prayer saves the _____. John 3:16

~Prayer builds _____ in the believer. Jude 20

~Prayer heals the _____. James 5:13-15

~With prayer we can receive _____. James 1:5

~With prayer we can receive _____. Philippians 4:5-7

~Prayer keeps one from _____. Matthew 26:41

~Prayer reveals the _____ of God. Luke 11:9-10

~Prayer brings _____ to God, the Father. John 14:13

~Prayer allows us to have _____ with God. Proverbs 15:8

Prayer is a privilege. As we look up these verses, discuss what they teach us about the privilege of prayer.

Psalm 34:17-18

Psalm 145:18

Hebrews 4:16

I Peter 3:12a

Why do we pray "in Jesus name"?

1. Jesus is the only way to the Father. John 14:6
2. Jesus is the only mediator between God and us. I Timothy 2:5
3. Jesus promises to give what we ask for in His name. If we are abiding in Christ, we can petition the Father with all the authority of Christ. We must ask in His name on the basis of Who He is, not in our own name on the basis of who we are. John 14:14

We've all heard the term, "prayer warrior". Why do you think this is a valid name for a person who prays?

Here are some additional things to think about when you are having your prayer time:

1. Come to the throne with reverence. God is the Almighty One. But have confidence that He desires to commutate with you.
2. Begin by thanking Him for the things He has done in your life. He doesn't need any reminders, but you will be blessed as you think on these past blessings.
3. Worship and praise Him for who He is and what that means to you.
4. Confess your failings and sins. Ask for and receive His forgiveness.
5. Ask for His guidance throughout this day. Commit the day to Him.
6. Present your body as a "Living sacrifice." (See Romans 12: 1-2)
7. Pray for others and well as your own needs.
8. Pray His will to be done most of all.
9. Tell Him you love Him.

A dear friend of mine once said that she didn't know what treasures God had in store for her, but she wanted everything He offered her. One of the precious treasures God offers us here on planet Earth is the privilege of communicating with Him by way of prayer. Accept the precious gift and talk to Him often!

Blessings!

# 19

# I AM THE I AM

Names identify who we are. In Biblical times, names defined the character or characteristics of a person. Joshua was known as Joshua, son of Nun because his father's name was Nun. James and John were called Sons of Thunder because of their quick and fierce temper. The emphasis put on names is not so common today. Do you know why you were given your name and what it means?

When we think of God we might think of Him as Father God or Creator God or the Almighty One. In the Old Testament, one of the most common names He was known by was Jehovah. The first time this name was used in the Bible was in Genesis 1:1 when it was used with an extra name to further describe His character, Jehovah—Elohim, meaning—God the Creator. The *him* on the end of the word Elohim is very important here because in the Hebrew language it is a plural ending meaning more than one. We know God as a triune God—Father, Son and Holy Spirit. So all three were in the beginning of the earth's creation.

Many times Jehovah was followed by one of His many characteristics such as Jehovah-Jireh, which means He is my provider. This name was first spoken by Abraham in Genesis 22 after God provided a ram for the burnt offering instead of Abraham offering his son, Isaac as the sacrifice.

We can still call on this name today because Jehovah-Jireh is still our Provider. The Lord's prayer says that we are to ask Him for our daily bread kind of like manna that was given fresh each morning to the Israelites in the wilderness. Wherever God's people are, He wants them to depend on Him for their daily needs. Why doesn't God just give us a year's supply of provisions instead of us asking Him daily for our needs?

What has been your experience in receiving God's provisions?

Have you ever had any unusual circumstances surrounding God's supplying your daily needs?

There is a promise in Philippians 4:19 which states that we can depend on God to supply all our needs. Let's look it up and write it here:

In order for us to claim this promise and every other promise in the Bible, we have to trust the One who promised. We have to settle in our minds that the One making the promise is first of all able to keep the promise and second that when we call on His name He will do the thing that will benefit us the most. We can't be wishy-washy here. He is the only One we trust with our best interests in mind. Look at Psalm 20:7.

Chariots and horses represent the power of men. Our trust rests upon God's provision and power. Have you learned to trust first and foremost in God? What are your thoughts?

Let's look at the list of God's names:

EL SHADDAI—The All-Sufficient One
EL ELYON—The God Most High
ADONAI—LORD, Master
JEHOVAH-NISSI—The Lord My Banner
ELOLAM—The Everlasting God
JEHOVAH-JIREH—The LORD Will Provide
YAHWEH—LORD, Jehovah
ELOHIM—The Creator
JEHOVAH-RAAH—The LORD My Shepherd
QANNA—Jealous

JEHOVAH-RAPHA—The LORD Who Heals
JEHOVAH-SHALOM—The LORD Is Peace
JEHOVAH-SHAMMAH—The LORD Is There
JEHOVAH-SABAOTH—The LORD of Hosts
EL ROI—The God Who Sees
JEHOVAH-TSIDKENU—The LORD Our Righteousness
JEHOVAH-MEKODDISHKEM—The LORD Who Sanctifies You

*"Those who know Your name will trust in You, for You, Lord, have never forsaken those who seek You."* (Psalm 9:10 NIV)

In a commentary I read on this verse it said that the phrase: who know Your name was the Old Testament equivalent of saving faith in the New Testament. And the phrase: have not forsaken is a further explanation of the meaning of God's name. He is a faithful God—a God who is always there and never gives up on His people.

Share how you feel about a God who is always there when you call and will never give up on you. Any examples you could share from your life experiences?

Jehovah-shammah is found in Ezekiel 48:35. There it is used in reference to the earthly Jerusalem, the city which the Lord Jesus Christ will inhabit when He returns to earth to reign as King of kings and Lord of lords. The name of the city from that day shall be known as "The LORD is there." The Hebrew word shammah simply means "there."

This information might not mean much to us now but the name Jehovah-shammah should be very meaningful. For us personally it means that wherever we go, Jehovah-shammah is there. There is no place that we go that God is not there. One of His unique character traits is that He is omnipresent . . . everywhere, all the time. This means that we, as God's children are never alone.

Because we are women of prayer and because a large part of our prayer ministry involves prayer for healing, the name of the God who heals should be one we are familiar with. That name is Jehovah-rapha. There are many hurting people all around us who need a healing touch from

Jehovah-rapha. Whether it is a physical infirmity or an illness of the mind or emotions, our great Physician has the power to bring forth a healing. It is up to Him in His infinite wisdom to decide how and if the healing will occur.

The name Jehovah-rapha was first recorded in Exodus 15 after God parted the Red Sea allowing the Israelites to escape from the Egyptians. They had been walking three days without finding water and had a cranky and grumbling attitude. God provided water and made a decree for them. Read what was said in Exodus 15:25-27.

Here are a few of the many instances where Jehovah-rapha's healing power was at work:

2 Chronicles 7:14 . . . What is our part in this promise?

Isaiah 53:5 . . . What can we learn from this scripture?

Psalm 147:3 . . . Jehovah-rapha is a healer of many kinds. What does this verse say He heals?

Think about the last time you needed healing. To whom did you go? What happened? Share if you will.

When we read about the Israelites and their lack of commitment to obey God's commands and compare that to today's world, we find that not a lot has changed in all that time. Our world even seems even more evil today if that's possible. But is it hopeless? I don't believe so.

Another name that God revealed to us through His word is Jehovah—tsidkenu, the Lord our righteousness. And with that revelation came the promise of a new covenant, the covenant of grace—and with it, a new heart. First read Jeremiah 31:31-34.

There is hope! We can be made right with God. Righteous is more than goodness, it is a right standing with God, to live according to His standards. But righteousness requires a new heart and we can have it because of Jehovah-tsidkenu, the Lord our righteousness.

The old covenant emphasis was on the _____. Under the new covenant, we experience _____. Under the new covenant, we no longer need intermediaries like priests or prophets to teach us about God. We can have a personal relationship with Him! Through Jesus' work on the cross as an atonement for our sins, we can experience hope for the future. We can have a new life and bring others into this new life. I know I've written it very simply here, but the message of Jehovah-tsidkenu is clear: God's desire for us is right standing with Him so that we may enjoy personal fellowship with Him now and forever!

Put yourself in Moses' place. He was standing in the field, tending sheep, far from any other human when he saw a strange thing. As he got closer he sees that . . . yes, it is a bush that seems to be burning but it's not burning up. Suddenly he hears a voice coming from the middle of the bush calling to him, "Moses, Moses!" He timidly answers, "Here I am" as he inches forward. "Don't come any closer and take your sandals off for you are standing on holy ground! I am the God of your father, the God of Abraham, Isaac, and Jacob." Pretty intense, right?

It seems that God has an important mission and He has specifically chosen Moses for the job . . . to bring God's people out of Egypt where they've been slaves for 400 years.

"I can't go, I've got these sheep to tend to", thinks Moses. "I certainly can't go back to Egypt. Who am I that I should talk to the Pharaoh about bringing the people out of Egypt? Who shall I say sent me? Why me God?" (Forgive my translation!)

Have you ever made excuses when God called you to do something? How did it turn out?

In Exodus 3:13-15 we find the conversation between God and Moses. Read it now. Has God ever impressed upon you to do something and you ignored the feeling? It never turns out for our benefit, does it?

Jehovah is the self-existent One—I AM WHO I AM. He is the eternal I AM, the Alpha and the Omega, the same yesterday, today, and forever. All of life is contained in Him. Why do we look elsewhere? Why do we not rest in His unchangeableness? He has never failed. Would He begin with me or you? He cannot. He is Jehovah, the self-existent, promise-keeping God.

An interesting note I found when researching this study is found in Matthew 14:27. This is what Jesus replied to the disciples when He was walking on the water toward their boat. Read it below from the AMP:

*"But instantly He spoke to them, saying, Take courage! I AM! Stop being afraid!"*

Jesus in the New Testament is calling Himself I AM which is one of God's names in the Old Testament. Something to pause and ponder, don't you think?

We've just had a little taste of the names of God and what they mean in today's study. Names are important. The more we learn of God's names, the more we know of Him.

Blessings!

NEXT

ir User ID and Password if you prefer.

Policy

manage a claim.

# 20

# FRET NOT THYSELF

*"¹Fret not thyself because of evildoers, neither be thou envious against the workers of iniquity. ²For they shall soon be cut down like the grass, and wither as the green herb.*

*³Trust in the LORD, and do good; so shalt thou dwell in the land, and verily thou shalt be fed. ⁴Delight thyself also in the LORD: and he shall give thee the desires of thine heart.*

*⁵Commit thy way unto the LORD; trust also in him; and he shall bring it to pass. ⁶And he shall bring forth thy righteousness as the light, and thy judgment as the noonday.*

*⁷Rest in the LORD, and wait patiently for him: fret not thyself because of him who prospereth in his way, because of the man who bringeth wicked devices to pass.*

*⁸Cease from anger, and forsake wrath: fret not thyself in any wise to do evil. ⁹For evildoers shall be cut off: but those that wait upon the LORD, they shall inherit the earth."* Psalm 37:1-9 (KJV)

Doesn't this passage of scripture seem to be saying, "Don't worry about what others do when you can't do anything about it anyway. Just be the person

God has shown you that He wants you to be." In other words—mind your own business! If you can just be patient, God will work it all out for your benefit and His glory!

As devoted followers of Jesus Christ, we have every reason to be patient in our trials of life. I can think of at least three:

1. We know God's in control. He's helped us before and there's no reason to think He won't do it again.
2. This isn't the first time we've had trouble and it won't be the last. The Bible says in fact, that we will have tribulation here on planet Earth. No surprise there!
3. We know the end of the story. We believers come out the winners if we are just patient and put our trust in the One who redeemed us! Do what you can do and let God do what you can't do!

How do you handle problems that you can't change?

In what ways are you more flexible as you have grown in the Lord?

What does attitude have to do with the way trials are resolved in your life?

What is the hardest area in your life to trust God with?

Look at Nehemiah 8:10.

You can find joy in the strength God gives you as you face the trials of this life. You might not be aware of joy at first because your mind is on your problem not on God. As soon as you focus on Him, you will feel joy bubbling up from deep within yourself, maybe slowly at first, but know this—the joy of the Lord is available waiting to minister and comfort you.

I have experienced this joy, so I know it is possible. Have you? Any examples or comments?

The Word says that in this life we will have many trials. The reality is then, that when this trial is over, another will probably crop up sometime in the near future. So if we know that trials will come and go in our lifetime, why do we waste precious time worrying over these earthy things?

I don't know the answer to that—but I do know that worrying and fretting over our circumstances is useless. And dear sisters, here's another reason not to worry: Stress and worry will eventually show up on our faces and that can give us one more thing to worry about . . . looking older than our years!

Worry means—to torment oneself with disturbing thoughts!

Striving to be an overcomer in our trials would give us many more benefits—and we would be at a place where we could feel the joy being offered to us by our kind heavenly Father. (I never said it would be easy!) Worrying is not a joyful practice. God cannot work in a negative atmosphere. Develop a positive outlook and watch Him work! Oh the joy of seeing Him work out difficult, messy, yucky circumstances on your behalf!

Outlook determines outcome. Choose to focus on God and good. See Proverbs 4:25-27.

Just imagine how our everyday life would change if we focused on God in all of our daily activities. Would we give any thought to what people think of us? Or how our deeds would be judged by those who witnessed them? Some of us worry about how we look to others—we don't want to offend anyone. Our goal should be how we look in God's eyes. Be a God pleaser not a people pleaser. Being Spirit-led is freedom. That gives us one area where we don't need to worry or fret.

**The antidote for worry is trust!**

Another popular area of worry is what's going to happen to me tomorrow? What if my husband cheats on me? What if my kids don't get good grades? What if I get in a car accident? Worrying about something that might happen is a waste of precious time. In fact, I read a report that said 99% of what we worry about won't happen anyway. Do birds worry? Do frogs worry? Then why do we?

**Worry is a down payment on the trouble you are never going to have!**

Sometimes we worry about things we cannot change. We refuse to accept life as it is. Some circumstances in life are fixed and we must do the best we can and not whine or complain. People often complain about the weather. There is not much any of us can do about the weather so worrying about it is useless. Someone has written these words:

> **After all, man is nothing but a fool,**
> **When it's hot, he wants it cool;**
> **When it's cool, he wants it hot;**
> **He always wants it the way it's not.**

When we learn to accept things we can not change, our lives will be much more peaceful and stress-free. Dwelling on those unchangeable things is a joy robber and we need to train ourselves to overlook them.

**Blessed are the flexible for they shall never be bent out of shape!**

Let's look again at Psalm 37 (at the top of the first page). In verse 3 we read . . . *"Trust in the Lord."*

Verse 4 . . . *"Delight thyself also in the Lord."*

Verse 5 . . . *"Commit thy way unto the Lord."*

And in verse 9 . . . *"those that wait upon the Lord, they shall inherit the earth."*

The time spent on earth is preparation time for heaven. If we spend all our time fretting how is that preparing us for spending eternity with God? Notice the words in the verses above . . . **trust, delight, commit** and **wait.** Those are the ideals we should set our minds on to live a God honored life here on planet Earth.

These phases all express faith and hope. There is no hopelessness when God is our focus. No situation is entirely desperate. A good verse to memorize is Psalm 37:5 which says . . . *"Commit your way unto the Lord; trust also in Him; and He shall bring it to pass."* (NKJV)

Do you believe that God can do the impossible? Maybe He can in the Bible but not in your circumstance? The word here is trust, sisters! Trust Him for those difficult moments because comfort and confidence comes from trusting in Him to work all things out for your good. If you think your present situation will turn out in a negative way, it probably will. Think victory and you are certain to experience that! Our hope is in the Lord, dear sisters. He is more than able to supply all we need.

In every situation in life, it is our attitude that makes the difference. It is a human response to worry. But we know from past experience that worrying doesn't get us anywhere. In order to live a victorious life, we must train ourselves to worry less and trust more. Not an easy task, but with God's help and our determination it can be accomplished. (Reread Luke 18:27)

**The greater we see our God; the smaller we see our problems!**

Blessings!

# 21

# BEING SURE

*"Now faith is **being sure** of what we hope for and certain of what we do not see."* Hebrews 11:1 NIV

There is a lot of uncertainty in this world we live in. There many decisions to be made through out our day and we wonder whether we are making the right choices. Some of our choices tend to be small, affect only us and not important in the bigger picture, like what to wear today. Others are more essential like our choice of attitude and words for instance. Decisions about how to handle situations and people are very important because people are made in God's image and they are eternal. God's goal is for everyone to someday live with Him in heaven, so He especially cares about how respectful and loving we treat His children.

If you have been treated harshly by a fellow believer, the best thing for you to do is to forgive that offense and move on. If you have treated another brother or sister unfairly, the best thing for you to do is to ask forgiveness of the person and of Father God and move on. The reason we need to take care of these matters quickly is that these are the things that Satan will use to his advantage and do as much damage as he's allowed to our faith walk. Agree or disagree? Any thoughts?

**"Get rid of your old baggage before Satan offers to help you carry it."**

There is an account in the book of John about Jesus, standing on shore, calling to His disciples who were out in the lake fishing. This happened early one morning just after His resurrection. The men were at loose ends after the loss of their beloved Leader, so they did what they commonly did before they met Jesus, they went fishing. John recognized Him and said, *"It is the Lord!"* Peter quickly jumped into the water, hurrying to shore to greet his Lord.

This had been a stressful and confusing time for the disciples and Jesus was gracious to appear before them and several others at different times before His ascension into heaven. He wanted to encourage them to continue to believe and walk in faith. While they were talking and eating breakfast around the campfire, Jesus focused on Peter to assure him of His love and forgiveness in the presence of His other disciples.

Peter as you know had denied knowing Jesus three times and now Jesus asked him three times about his love and loyalty. (John 21) To each of Peter's affirmatives, Jesus relied, to Peter, *"Feed My sheep."* We can come to the conclusion that Jesus was showing confidence in Peter's faith and commitment to his role of shepherding the church as they waited on Christ's return to earth.

When we read the two books of the Bible that Peter was responsible for writing, we can see that he took the role of shepherding God's people very seriously. Sometimes we need that crisis of faith to make us determined to stay the course. Philippians 2:12 tells us to: *"work out your salvation with fear and trembling."* (NKJV) Yes, salvation is a free gift. No, we should never take it for granted and always be mindful of the great cost.

Here is what Peter, the "shepherd" of Christ's sheep, gives us as guidelines on developing Christian character and how to live 'til Christ's return found in 2 Peter 1:2-11: NLT

[2] *May God give you more and more grace and peace as you grow in your knowledge of God and Jesus our Lord.*

[3] *By his divine power, God has given us everything we need for living a godly life. We have received all of this by coming to know him, the one who called us to*

*himself by means of his marvelous glory and excellence. [4] And because of his glory and excellence, he has given us great and precious promises. These are the promises that enable you to share his divine nature and escape the world's corruption caused by human desires.*

*[5] In view of all this, make every effort to respond to God's promises. Supplement your faith with a generous provision of moral excellence, and moral excellence with knowledge, [6] and knowledge with self-control, and self-control with patient endurance, and patient endurance with godliness, [7] and godliness with brotherly affection, and brotherly affection with love for everyone.*

*[8] The more you grow like this, the more productive and useful you will be in your knowledge of our Lord Jesus Christ. [9] But those who fail to develop in this way are shortsighted or blind, forgetting that they have been cleansed from their old sins.*

*[10] So, dear brothers and sisters, work hard to prove that you really are among those God has called and chosen. Do these things, and you will never fall away. [11] Then God will give you a grand entrance into the eternal Kingdom of our Lord and Savior Jesus Christ.*

In verse 2 what two blessings are we given as we grow in faith?

Since our knowledge of Jesus grows as we mature in the faith, we will experience His grace and peace on many different occasions in our daily walk with Him. What has been your experience?

I really like verse 3 since it states that God has given us every spiritual thing we need for a tremendous walk of faith here on planet Earth. In Philippians 4:13 it talks about doing *"all things through Him who strengthens me."* (NKJV) There are conditions though; we must first accept Him into our lives, giving Him access into our daily thoughts and actions. We must have a personal relationship with Him, not just head knowledge of who He is. And finally, we must love Him enough to desire to do everything according to His plan and purpose. That is the blueprint for a victorious life.

It seems like a hard thing to give up all our ideas and plans to follow His ideas and plans doesn't it? I guess that's the beginning of faith. Faith grows when we give Him liberty in all areas of our lives. Bits and pieces at first, then as we see Him doing great things, the trust level allows us to give Him more and more of ourselves. And pretty soon our lives are so connected to Him that we wouldn't think of doing things without His input. That's growing in faith.

Verse 4 is all about the promises of divine provision found in the Bible. If you are anxious and fearful, Jesus promises peace. (John 14:27) Are you feeling lonely and without friends? Jesus promises to be your friend. (John 15:15) Do you feel guilty and need forgiveness? Jesus promised that *"if we confess our sins, He is faithful and just to forgive us our sins and to cleanse us from all unrighteousness."* (1 John 1:9 NKJV) These are only a few promises we have access to. Peter called them *"very great and precious promises."*(verse 4) What are some other promises?

Verses 5-7 are like a stairs made up of virtues which lead to the greatest virtue-love. We are be seriously committed to grow our faith by seeking goodness, knowledge, self-control, perseverance, godliness, brotherly kindness and love. All of these character traits are Christ-like and come from choosing to obey the promptings of the Holy Spirit who lives in us.

The presence of these qualities in a Christian is a guarantee of a healthy, fruitful, and God honoring life. The lack of fruitfulness could be caused by two things: blindness or forgetfulness. (verses 8-9) We must be aware of things of eternal value and not just busy ourselves with earthly things. Planet Earth is just a preparation for eternal life in heaven!

Being sure of your faith is a pretty serious matter, a matter of eternal life or death. We must know the truth and live accordingly. Peter wrote to the church to clear up some false teaching and the difficulties it caused. We also must be aware of false teaching. If you have a question or an unsettled feeling that something doesn't ring true, go to the Word or ask someone you respect or even bring it up in a Bible study setting if it pertains to the study.

Many times people just accept what is taught to them and never look it up for themselves. Second hand knowledge doesn't grow faith. It is to our benefit to have an active curiosity about everything concerning God and His life principles and commands. He wants us to live a victorious life and we can if we follow His guidelines for holy living. The great motivation for us is the soon coming return of Christ and the punishment and rewards that will follow. The account of the ten virgins makes it clear that if we are not ready, there won't be any time for us to prepare. (Matthew 25)

There is work to be done sisters. We can't be saved and then sit back and relax. If we are to grow and mature in our faith, it will take lots of time and effort on our part. Not easy, but certainly not a drudgery.

Blessings!

# 22

# PRAYING GOD'S WORD . . . SPEAKING TO GOD WITH THE MOST BEAUTIFUL WORDS IN THE WORLD—HIS!

God has given us the wonderful gift of His essence in written form. It is one of the ways in which we can know Him. Many of us have several translations of the Bible in our homes. I think they are to be used to the full benefit in every aspect of our spiritual life. I don't know if God ever intended for us to pray His words back to Him, but why can't we use His beautiful words when we communicate with Him? After all, they are also the most powerful words in the world!

Ever wonder why people who pray are called "prayer warriors"? In Ephesians 6, Paul talks about putting on the full armor of God. In verse 17, he tells us to take *"the sword of the Spirit which is the Word of God."* (NKJV) Scripture is called the sword of the Spirit because it is inspired by the Holy Spirit. It is also the only weapon of defense in the armor of God. The use of Scripture in prayer warfare (and believe me, praying is spiritual warfare) is a work of the Holy Spirit. He brings it to your memory as you pray. Psalm

119:11 says *"I have hidden Your Word in my heart that I might not sin against You."* (NIV)

The Holy Spirit gives us the needed power to fight against Satan as we pray. Satan cannot stand against the Word of God when it is used in the power of the Spirit. Jesus, remember, silenced Satan with the Word, and so can we when we wield the sword of the Spirit. Look at how Jesus defeated His enemy in Matthew 4:1-11.

Have you ever used scripture to fight your enemies? (Like temptation, depression, loneliness, discouragement, etc.) Share your experience if you can.

Nothing makes the devil more nervous than a child of God on her knees! Here are some powerful words you can use in your prayer time: These words are not only powerful, they will be beautiful sounds to God's ears.

Yes Lord!

Your will be done.

Here I am, use me.

I pray in the name of Jesus.

Thank You Lord!

I love You Father God.

These are powerful words, write them down. Use them. Can you think of any other examples?

Paul tells us in that last part of Ephesians 6 ... *"With all prayer and petition, pray at all times in the Spirit and with this in view, be on the alert with all perseverance and petition for all the saints."* (verse 18 NASB)

Not something we should be taking lightly. Pray boldly with a holy boldness.

Here are some examples of how to pray God's Word back to Him:

Psalm 100:4-5—

*"Enter into His gates with thanksgiving, and into His courts with praise. Be thankful to Him, and bless His name. For the LORD is good; His mercy is everlasting, and His truth endures to all generations."* (NKJV)

You can pray these verses like this:

Lord, I enter Your gates with thanksgiving, this morning my heart is filled with praise. I thank You and praise Your name for You have been so good and faithful to me. Your love has so surrounded me! Oh, I thank You and praise You!

Such a paraphrase of God's Word prepares your heart for praise and worship of Him.

Another example:

1 Peter 1:8—

*"Though you have not seen Him, you love Him; and even though you do not see Him now, you believe in Him and are filled with an inexpressible and glorious joy."* (NIV)

As you read this verse, you can pause and lift your heart to God and say something like this:

Father,

Even though I cannot see You with my natural eyes, I can feel Your presence all about me. I believe You are working on my behalf and I love You. I know that I will see You one day in Heaven and that fills my heart with such joy that I can't even find the words. The thoughts of You fill me with a joy beyond words! Praise Your wonderful name!

Another example:

Psalm 19:14 NIV—

*"May the words of my mouth and the meditation of my heart be acceptable in Your sight, O Lord, my Rock and my Redeemer."*

This is one I use every morning and helps me through the day, because if my words and my thoughts are acceptable to God, then my day will go a lot smoother. If you are a sister who, like me, has trouble with the mouth, this is a very useful prayer!

An example to help you to powerfully pray for the salvation of others is to use their name in the scripture. Fill in the blanks with your loved one's name.

John 3:16—

"I pray that You, Father, so loved _____ that You gave Your only begotten Son, that if _____ believes in Him _____ should not perish but have everlasting life."

Prayer is the foundation of all that we do in our service for Christ. Part of the foundation of a building or house is not seen, but it's important to the safety and well being of the people who live and work in those buildings.

Can you see how using God's Word in our prayers can build a strong foundation to our prayer life?

Prayer is also about building a relationship with God. It strengthens our faith when we see prayers being answered; it helps us to automatically turn things over to God. And it makes us more in tune with His Word and His promises. We become partners in Kingdom building with Him.

There is a beautiful prayer in 3John 2 that you could pray for any friend or loved one. Look it up and write below, and fill in the name of the person you are praying for.

Look up the following verses and write a short prayer using God's words.

2 Thessalonians 3:16

Romans 12:1-2

Psalm 103:17-18

I Corinthians 15:58

As you study your Bible look for verses to change into prayers. Write them in a notebook for further study. Make using God's words in your prayers a practice. You will be blessed and so will our Heavenly Father.

One last salvation verse:

Ezekiel 11:19 AMP—

"And I will give _____ one heart (new heart) and I will put a new spirit within _____; and I will take the stony (unnaturally hardened) heart out of _____s flesh and will give _____ a heart of flesh (sensitive and responsive to the touch of _____'s God.)

There are many ways to pray. This way of speaking God's words back to Him is just one. Just don't forget the main idea and that is to pray. And pray consistently, believing that God will answer.

Blessings!

# 23

# DON'T SWEAT THE SMALL STUFF

Isn't it amazing how it's the littlest thing that finally drives us over the edge? We are minding our own business when some rude person crowds in front of us. Or someone says the wrong thing at the wrong time. Or the kids ask you for a treat when you've said no for about the hundredth time. Or we worry about the gas prices, which will affect the food prices and in turn affect the . . . . and on and on until our stress level is completely out of control!

God's Word has lots of advice on how to reduce the stress in our lives. Here's one from Matthew 6:34 NKJV:

*"Therefore do not worry about tomorrow, for tomorrow will worry about its own things. Sufficient for the day is its own trouble."*

Never borrow from the future. If you worry about what may happen tomorrow and it doesn't happen, you have worried in vain. Even if it does happen, you have to worry twice.

**THE ANTIDOTE FOR WORRY IS TRUST!**

Here are some simple ways to keep the little things of life from robbing you of your sanity and bring you peace and contentment in the stressful world we live in:

## CHRISTIAN WAYS TO REDUCE STRESS

1. **Pray** ~ Pretty basic isn't? Why do we try everything in our power and then remember to pray? God is the God of the big and the small. He is interested in everything about us.
   How will our lives change if we are continually plugged into His power?
2. **Go to bed on time.** ~ At this stage of our lives, we probably know how much sleep we need to keep us functioning at acceptable levels. We have a way of stressing over the littlest thing if we are sleep deprived.
3. **Get up on time so you can start the day unrushed.** ~ Getting up late usually means we also get up on the wrong side of the bed. Watch out family! Let's not raise their stress levels either!
4. **Say No to projects that won't fit into your time schedule or that will compromise your mental health.** ~ Can you say no without feeling guilty? If you know the plan and purpose God has for you, it won't be difficult to say no to the things that don't fit in with those plans and purposes.
5. **Delegate tasks to capable others.** ~ How good are you at this on a scale of 1 (I would rather to it myself than bother anyone else) to 10 (I know you can handle this without my help!) Remember Martha and her sister Mary? Review their story in Luke 10:38-42.
6. **Simplify and unclutter your life.** ~ Look at Hebrews 12:1
   Why do you think having stuff and being busy can lead to sin?
7. **Less is more. (Although one is often not enough, two are often too many.)** ~ A life principle says that the more stuff you have, the more time it takes to care for it. Do you agree?
8. **Allow extra time to do things and to get to places**. ~ Besides being a stress-builder, this habit will make us continually late. Being late is a discourtesy to those who have to wait for you and a dishonor to your Heavenly Father. Do you agree or disagree with the last statement?
9. **Pace yourself.** ~ Spread out big changes and difficult projects over time; don't lump the hard things all together.
10. **Take one day at a time**. ~ Look at Matthew 6:34 (at the top of first page)
11. **Separate worries from concerns**. If a situation is a concern, find out what God would have you do and let go of the anxiety. If you can't do anything about a situation, forget it.

> **God grant me the serenity
> to accept the things I cannot change;
> courage to change the things I can;
> and wisdom to know the difference**

12. **Live within your budget**. ~ Don't use credit cards for ordinary purchases.
13. **Have backups**.~ an extra car key in your wallet, an extra house key buried in the garden, extra stamps, etc. ~ Taking these steps will reduce the stress level considerably and it's so simple to do.
14. **K.M.S. (Keep Mouth Shut).~** This single piece of advice can prevent an enormous amount of trouble. ~ To reach success with this piece of advice, we all probably need a lot of prayer and fasting! Look at Ephesians 4:29 and then at Proverbs 25:11.
15. **Do something for the Kid in You everyday**. ~ What is one of your fun, favorite things to do?
    When was the last time you did it?
16. **Carry a Bible with you to read while waiting in line.**
17. **Get enough rest**. ~ See #2 and #3
18. **Eat right**.
19. **Get organized so everything has its place**. ~ There are many ways to manage your day and to retrieve some of the time wasters that seem to be a part of every day. Keep your eyes open for ways to reduce your stress level and still take good care of your home and family. Discover small changes that will help you function better. Allow God to be in the details of your day. Practice being in His presence as you do the necessary things to make your home and life run smooth. Doing that will add richness to the quality of your life.
    The reason for us to be organized in our daily lives is found in John 9:4. What is the reason?
20. **Listen to a tape while driving that can help improve your quality of life.**
21. **Write down thoughts and inspirations.** You'll be glad you did when you read them later on.
22. **Every day, find time to be alone.**
23. **Having problems? Talk to God on the spot**. ~ Try to nip small problems in the bud. Don't wait until it's time to go to bed to try and pray.
24. **Make friends with Godly people**. ~ Everyone needs a support group. If you can't find a Bible study to join, start one.

25. **Keep a folder of favorite scriptures on hand**. ~ What is one of your favorite verses? Why?
26. **Remember that the shortest bridge between despair and hope is often a good "Thank you, Jesus!"** ~ A grateful spirit is a stress reducer because the more we express our gratitude, the more we are blessed! See Hebrews 12:28.
27. **Laugh.**
28. **Laugh some more!**
29. **Take your work seriously, but not yourself at all.**
30. **Develop a forgiving attitude (most people are doing the best they can).** ~ See Matthew 18:21-22 and discuss what Jesus meant.
31. **Be kind to unkind people (they probably need it the most).** ~ Kindness is one of the Fruit of the Spirit. We all have the kindness gene in us when the Holy Spirit is living inside us. A good principle for this is found in Matthew 7:12.
32. **Sit on your ego.** ~ Someone you encounter may feel the need to be served first or park in the spot you were waiting for—let them. And extent grace. They are needier than you, because you are a child of the King! (a princess!!) God gave us a promise for grace in 2 Corinthians 12:9.
33. **Talk less; listen more.**
34. **Slow down.** ~ Don't just be busy, be fruitful! See Colossians 1:10
35. **Remind yourself that you are not the general manager of the universe**. ~ Someone Else already has that job and He's not retiring!
36. **Every night before bed, think of one thing you're grateful for that you've never been grateful for before**.

When we stress about daily things that won't even matter in 6 months from now, our minds and even our bodies become tired. As Christ followers, we are truly blessed to be able to turn that stressful stuff over to God. It's a learned response. Trusting God with our stuff is not easy at first, but in time and with practice, it will become a welcome habit.

(This study was inspirited by a e-mail I got from a friend called, "Christian Ways to Reduce Stress". Author unknown. I enjoyed putting in the comments and scripture!)

When we can release our concerns to Him, we will experience the "quietness and confidence" (see Isaiah 30:15) that comes from a life of faith in the one who created us.

**We mutter and sputter, we fume and we spurt;**
**We mumble and grumble, our feelings get hurt;**
**We can't understand things, our vision grows dim,**
**When all that we need is communion with Him!**
**Author unknown**

Blessings!

# 24

# MARY, MARTHA AND ME

Once upon a time there were two sisters who lived together along with their brother in a small country village. These sisters were quite different from each other in personality. Mary was quiet, a deep thinker and possessed spiritual insight. Mary loved the Lord with all her heart. Martha was a caregiver, very organized, and possessed the gift of hospitality. She also loved the Lord. For two women living in the same house, these women got along pretty well, most of the time.

An example of their differences in personality would be if the sisters heard about a friend or neighbor who was sick, Martha would cook and bake delicious treats and clean their house for them. Mary would sit and hold their hand and whisper words of encouragement to them. Most of the time, they complemented each other's strengthens and weaknesses.

One day they were expecting their valued friend and spiritual teacher to visit them. They were both excited to see Him as He didn't visit that often. Martha practically wore herself out getting the house ready for His visit. Mary went for a leisurely walk to ponder all His previous teachings. Both were preparing for His coming in her own way.

You've probably already guessed that these sisters are the Mary and Martha of the Bible. The beginning of their story is found in Luke 10:38-42. Let's read it together.

What do you see as Martha's major positive characteristic?

When would making sure others were comfortable and felt welcomed <u>not</u> be a positive characteristic?

The gift of hospitality is an important one. It is a spiritual gift given to some believers to encourage and build up the rest of the body of believers. I appreciate that gift when I am warmly received into a sister's home and know she has cared enough to make things attractive and pleasant for my visit.

In this passage, Martha needed a sense of balance and it's a lesson we can learn from her behavior. We too can easily let our priorities get out of whack. During the past week, have you spent most of your time and energy seeking God's voice or in accomplishing your own everyday stuff? I think the balance here would be letting God into your everyday stuff. I know when I do that the day goes much smoother.

Get into the habit of involving God in all aspects of your day. Instead of turning things over in your mind, turn them over to God in prayer. Instead of worrying about the next decision, ask God to give you wisdom. Pray about things big and small. He is interested in our lives and wants to hear from you. Give Him free reign in your life.

Look at Psalm 73:28

This verse tells us that it is good to be _____ to God.

Look at Psalm 5:3

This verse tells when—_____ _____ _____.

Let's go back to Luke 10:38-42 and read it again.

What is the first characteristic of Mary that you see in this passage?

What is Jesus' opinion of her actions? (v.42)

To sit at Jesus' feet and listen to His teaching with the men was not a common practice among the women of that day. A woman's place was to serve the men and keep out of the way. Women were mostly viewed as a non-person. In fact, Jewish men in those days thanked God every morning in their prayers that He had created them "not as a slave, nor a heathen, nor a woman". ☹

Jesus was different than other men. He had introduced a new respect for women. He offered possibilities and opportunities unknown to women before that time. Mary felt completely at ease in His presence. The purpose of her existence had become clear in listening to His teachings.

Psalm 25:14 NLT:

*"Friendship with God is reserved for those who reverence Him. With them alone He shares the secrets of His promises."*

This was the "better thing that Mary had chosen." Martha missed the point as she was distracted in the busyness of the day. We must let nothing keep us from growing our relationship with God. If we follow that precept our short time on planet Earth will be blessed and our eternity will be certain.

As we can see in the "sister story", we all tend to have strengths and weaknesses. It's a good idea to know our weaknesses so we don't waste our time trying to do things we're not very good at. It is also good to know our strengths so we can concentrate on working on those things so we can be of better use to our Heavenly Father. It gives us confidence to know what we are good at. God has gifted each one of us in certain areas that are unique to us. It would be a shame to go through life not knowing and developing those gifts.

Take a few minutes and list 5 of your strengths and 5 weaknesses:

STRENGTHS

1.
2.
3.
4.
5.

WEAKNESSES

1.
2.
3.
4.
5.

Don't be afraid to admit what you can't do. It's good to know the things you can avoid and be more successful in doing the things you have strengths and gifts in. For instance, I don't have a good singing voice. It would be silly of me to think I could sing a solo or join the worship team. I would be wasting my time no matter how much I practiced. (I am a great appreciator of good music, that's why I don't sing too loud in public!)

However, one of my strengths is to study God's Word. I have been faithful to learn what the Word says about many different topics over the last 30 years. Because of that God has given me the ability to write out these Bible studies. In this way, He is using me to educate and encourage my sisters in the faith. Can you see how knowing your strengths and weaknesses can give you purpose in life? Knowing and revealing your strengths is not bragging on yourself—it is bragging on your Creator!

In Sunday school class, we've been studying about who we are in Christ. There is no greater confidence builder then knowing what God thinks about you. Here are just a few things that God says about you in His Word:

Matthew 5:13-14:
I am the _____ of the earth and the _____ of the world.

John 15:5:
I am a branch of the true _____, Jesus.

John 15:15-16:
"I have been chosen to _____ fruit."

Acts 1:8:
I am a personal, Spirit-empowered _____ for Christ.

1 Corinthians 3:16:
"I am a _____ of God."

2 Corinthians 6:1:
"I am God's _____."

Ephesians 2:10:
"I am God's _____, created to do good works."

Philippians 4:13:
"I can do all things _____ Christ who _____ me."

Think of it sisters, these are just some of the things that God thinks about each one of us! We are not made to be like the Bible characters we read about in the Word. Their stories are written there for us to use as an example and an encouragement for our lives.

We are not made to be like each other either. God gave us all different gifts so we can develop and use those gifts to help each other and to spread the good news of salvation for all who will believe. God made us to be us and He had given us a rich treasure chest of resources to help us to become a better us.

Blessings!

# 25

# FAN THE FLAME

When my granddaughter, Amanda, was 5 years old, John and I visited them one summer. They lived in an apartment complex in Fort Collins, CO that had a pool. Mandy loved to play in the water. She still does today. She was a little 5 year old social butterfly, flitting from one group of friends and activities to another. But playing in the pool was one of her very favorite things. So much so that she never gave a thought to the rules and the consequences of not obeying them.

There was a rope across the pool about a third of the way to the end. That rope signified the deeper part of the pool . . . the area for bigger and more experienced swimmers. Being the wonderful grandma that I am, I pointed that rope out to her before she jumped in and carefully explained its purpose.

She shook her head like she heard me, eager to join her friends, already in the pool. "Of course I know what that rope is for Grandma, and silly you for thinking you needed to remind me." She didn't say that of course, but I'm sure that's what she was thinking, if indeed her 5 year old brain comprehended anything other than . . . when can I join my friends in the pool?

Into the pool she went laughing and splashing, wanting to make up for lost time. I grabbed my chair and my book and went to join the other ladies, poolside. While the water looked cool and inviting, who wants to be in there with fifteen laughing and splashing kids? (Sweethearts, every one!)

I no more than settled in my chair, when I looked over to check on my little angel and realized she was already passed the rope and was in the bigger and more experienced swimmers area of the pool. Not wanting to yell and give the impression that I was a screaming, controlling kind of grandma, I sweetly call her to come over to me.

I calmly reminded her of the rules we discussed and she agreed that she had forgotten about the rope and why it was important. So just to instill in her the consequences of not obeying the rules and being a Grandma that likes to teach lessons as the occasions arise, I gave her a "time out" of 5 minutes. After I explained what a "time out" was, she responded, "But Grandma, if I sit here with you, I'll be missing the fun of swimming with my friends!" BINGO!

Sometimes the Holy Spirit calls us for a "time out". There are times when we get so wrapped up with the busyness of the day and we don't take the time to involve Him in our plans. At other times we may make a decision and don't have a peace about it. It may be that the Holy Spirit is checking us to reconsider that decision. He is very interested in our choices. His desire for us is to make the right ones. We all need time outs occasionally, no matter how old we are.

On that day at the pool, I was grateful that Mandy was obedient and took that 5 minutes to selah (pause and ponder) her actions. When the Holy Spirit calls us into a time out, we are wasting the opportunity if we pout and stew. We must consider it a learning opportunity and go on from there.

One of the daily choices we as Christian women make is: what shall I do today with my time, talents and treasure? If we are women with a growing family, the responsibilities of that is a given. If we work outside the home, we know that it takes up a major part of our day. But believe it or not, we all have an amount of time we can call our own.

Some of us like to spend time with our sisters. Oh! The joy of being in the sisterhood of the sisters! That time can be a wonderful resting, healing time for some. At other times, it can be a time of giving and sharing yourself with others who need your encouraging touch, words and prayers. Or it can be a fun time to laugh and just be. God wants us to have all of those experiences and more. It's part of life.

If we are in tune with God, He will show us what to do with our time, through the Holy Spirit's leading. The choice to follow God's leading, even though we may have our own agenda, comes from our desire to love and honor Him and be transformed into the image of His Son, Jesus. See 2 Corinthians 3:18.

This means that every time we give up our desire to do God's desire, we are being transformed from _____ to _____ or bit by bit. Every time we follow the Holy Spirit's urging we are fanning the flame of our love and commitment to our Heavenly Father. Every time we use our time, talents and treasure for God's purposes, it has eternal value. God gave us these gifts for a reason and one day we'll be asked to give an account of how we used them.

Look at 2 Timothy 1:6.

Another way of saying "fan the flame" is to be stirred up. Remember when you first said yes to Jesus? How you were so excited and drank in everything about Jesus, love, spiritual gifts, etc. that you could get your hands on? Maybe that was a while ago and you've cooled off a little. This is when you have to stir yourself up again. God deserved nothing less.

What are some ways you can fan the flame of your faith?

1.
2.
3.

The word picture of being "stirred up" is like a fire that has died down a little and is rekindled with a stick. The stirring causes the sparks to fly as the fire flames up and burns with new energy. Our Christian walk is not meant to be mediocre. It is intended to burn so brightly, that we send out sparks that will ignite spiritual fire in those around us!

The wonderful gifts of grace given to us by the Holy Spirit are called our spiritual gifts. We all have been given at least one. I don't think that any of us use our gifts to their full potential. A gift is a gift only after it's been received. We are richly blessed when we receive and use the gifts God has so graciously given to us. The greatest hindrance to not using the gifts as God intended for them to be used is _____! You guess it-fear!

Read together Matthew 25:14-25. (key verse is 25)

### FEAR: False Evidence Appearing Real!

Fear is not from God. He has given us power over fear. See 2 Timothy 1:7. We are delivered from the spirit of fear and in its place is power, (courage) and love and a sound mind (a quietness of mind).

If you are afraid to step out and use the gifts of time, talent and treasure that God has so freely given you, concentrate on the love He has for you and your love for Him. There is a wonderful scripture in 1 John 4:18. Read it and fill in the blanks.

*"There is _____ _____ in _____. But perfect _____ drives out _____."*(NIV)

If you could accomplish anything for God this week and know that you would have complete success, what would it be?

We followers of Christ have different personalities, gifts, interests and callings. What brings us all in a spirit of unity is our love for God. His purpose for each of us is as unique as we are. Sometimes the fire within us needs to be stirred up and fanned into a bright, burning flame full of purpose and determination. (Yes, I'm talking to you!) If you feel your love for the Father fading, quickly light the match that will rekindle that love. We're talking about a life of abundance and an eternity with Him. Mediocrity might get us into Heaven, but a Christian life full of excellence surely will!

Erma Bombeck was a wonderful Christian woman who is with Jesus now. She had this to say about her life:

**When I stand before God at the end of my life, I would hope that I would not have a single bit of talent left and could say, "I used everything You gave me."**

Oh! That we would be able to say that when we are about to enter there from here!

Blessings!

# 26

# GRACE! GRACE! GRACE!

How easy is it for you to extent grace on daily basis? Putting others before yourself. Not taking offense at unkind or thoughtless words or actions. People cutting you off on the road. Many unexpected things occur that can make or unmake our day and change our good mood to a bad mood.

When my daughter, Mary and I attended a Women's Conference a few years ago, one thing the group of ladies were encouraged to do was to spread grace all around. The way we were to remind ourselves to do this was to spread our hands and fingers out like we were sprinkling seeds and say: "Grace, Grace, Grace."

It was a good thing to learn because the plane trip home gave us plenty of opportunities to practice our skills! Those of you, who have ever traveled by air, know that the control of everything that happens is completely out of your control. You have no say in the time you leave, the time you arrive, the persons sitting next to you, the weather, the air traffic, the lack of comfort and courtesy extended to you. Nothing! It is one of the best times to practice the art of spreading grace.

Realize that it is a choice to extend grace, but more than that, it is a sacrifice of praise to the One who extended grace to us in the first place.

Definition of grace from the Bible dictionary:

**"Undeserved favor, especially that kind or degree of favor bestowed upon sinners through Jesus Christ."**

Shorter version:

**GRACE—God's Riches At Christ's Expense**

Look at 2 Corinthians 9:8.

Who can claim the benefits in this verse?

This verse states that God is able to make His grace abound toward us so that we can accomplish many things. This fact should make us all extremely happy and enabled to do every good work. Why is it then that so many Christians aren't living a life of joyous fulfillment? List some hindrances.

1.
2.
3.

Ephesians 1 lists many of the spiritual blessings and benefits we have in Christ. This one chapter alone should make it clear to us how much God loves us and wants to bestow grace and favor on us. Scan this scripture and name several benefits to us as God's children.

Reading all these benefits might make us seem like Wonder Woman and that we can do it all but James 4:6 remind us that *"God resists the proud, but gives grace to the humble"* (NKJV) God will work in us and through us as long as we aren't so full of ourselves that there is no room for Him. We need humble attitudes, knowing that only *"through Christ can we do all things."* (see Phil. 4:13)

Look at 2 Corinthians 12:7-9. Specifically note and underline in your Bible the words, *"My grace is sufficient for you . . ."*

My children are grown now but I can relate to mothers of young children when they have to walk pass the candy aisle at the grocery store. Some mothers don't handle those situations very well and some kids know the buttons to push. I was fortunate to not have too many problems in that area, but we all realize that it can be a situation of frustration for both the mom and the child.

What one thing do you want that you've never received? How did you react to this?

Why do you think God sometimes tells us no?

Are there any specific things you can do to be content with God's grace when he denies a request? If so, what are they?

Go back again to 2 Corinthians 12:7-9. Why was the "thorn" given to Paul (v. 7)?

What was God's response to Paul's request (v. 9)? How did Paul react to God's response?

Do you think you would have reacted like this? Explain.

Look at Philippians 4:6-7.

What should our attitude toward anxiety be, according to verse 6?

What are we supposed to do instead of worrying?

What should accompany our request?

If we follow the instructions in verse 6, what will the results be (v.7)?

Psalm 84:11AMP—*"For the Lord God is a Sun and Shield; the Lord bestows grace and favor and (future) glory (honor, splendor, and heavenly bliss)! No good thing will He withhold from those who walk uprightly."*

What a wonderful gift God's grace is! It is through His love for us that it is given. It is through our love for Him and knowledge of Him that we receive it. There are two things He expects us to do with this blessing of grace. The first one is found in 2 Peter 3:18. It is to:

As we pursue with passion and purpose our walk of faith and experience His grace in many unexpected places, the second thing He desires of us is to be gracious to others. It's actually God's grace that we are passing on when we forget the unkind words and deeds of others. It's His grace that covers unwelcome trials and delays in our organized day. His grace to us is our opportunity to extend grace to others.

If we can remember that we are on planet Earth for such a small speck of time compared to eternity, how easy it should be to will ourselves to throw out those "seeds of grace" and spread His love around. In the bigger picture, thoughtless words and deeds of others just don't matter.

God's desire for us is to grow in His grace and to pass it on. I pray that is your passion too!

Blessings!

## 27

# LISTEN TO YOUR COACH

Several years ago when I had knee joint replacement surgery, I had to assign a friend to be my designated coach. My husband, John got the assignment and it was his job to help me do my therapy before and after I left the hospital. He had to walk beside me (literally) as I walked down the hall and help me to remember all the exercises I needed to do. His job was to encourage me to do everything needed to get back on my feet again. And believe me when I tell you that he took his responsibilities very seriously. Sometimes I just wanted to bop him one! But I'm so glad now that he kept me on track.

I've been hearing lately, maybe you have too, about Life Coaches, especially among the rich and famous people. I'm not sure what all they do, but I have a feeling that they get paid pretty well for doing it.

Aren't you glad that you already have a Life Coach? If you are a Christ follower, you have a Life Coach, living inside of you. His name is the Holy Spirit.

The first reference to the Holy Spirit is made in Genesis 1:2. His influence is implied throughout the Old Testament, but His activities become more prominent in the New Testament. After Jesus ascended to be at the right hand of the Father, He sent the Holy Spirit to be the _____ or _____. Look at John 14:26 and 15:26. Another one of the Holy Spirit's functions is to be our _____. He is called to be the "one who walks along beside" every believer of Jesus Christ.

The Holy Spirit is interested in transforming us from the inside out. He is at work in lots of different ways, some of them supernatural. (After all, He is God!) He desires to show us the Father's will and steer us in the right direction. He provides the dynamics necessary for experiencing joy, peace, patience and contentment in spite of our circumstances. That's some Life Coach!

The Holy Spirit is a person, the third person of the Trinity; Father, Son and Holy Spirit. Three in One should not be foreign to us. Consider the pretzel. (Or the apple, or the egg.) All have three parts that are individual, but make one.

What are some benefits we receive through the Holy Spirit's indwelling in us? Look at these scriptures:

Romans 8:2:
John 16:13:
Acts 1:8:
Ephesians 1:13-14:
Romans 8:26-27:

In 1 Corinthians 3:16 we read that we are God's temple and that the Holy Spirit is living in us. Does knowing that make you want to act any differently? How?

John 14:26 says that the Holy Spirit will remind us of the things Jesus has said. This means to me that the words we read in the Bible and even the things He has spoken to us in prayer and through other people, He will remind us about at appropriate times. I am especially happy for this blessing since I seem to be more challenged to remember things as the days go by.

We've all had times when just the perfect scripture has come to our mind at the most opportune moment.

We don't have to know the Scripture word perfect and where it's found in the Bible for it to become powerful in the circumstance! We can count on God to fill in the blanks.

Look at Ephesians 5:18.

We know that the Holy Spirit comes to dwell in every believer. (I Corinthians 3:16) Why then are we commanded to "be filled with the Spirit"?

It is my understanding that while we have been sealed with the Holy Spirit as a mark of ownership, (Ephesians 1:13) as a believer of Jesus Christ, the filling of the Holy Spirit is a moment by moment action.

While we may not understand all the workings of the Holy Spirit in our lives, we can certainly agree that we are blessed by the Almighty God that has provided the power and the confidence He brings to our lives.

I believe that we are not using all the power available to us by the indwelling of the Holy Spirit. If we were then many of the issues we face would not be obstacles to overcome. We would no longer fear talking to others about salvation. We would be confident in using our spiritual gifts. We would feel secure in the knowledge of God's love for us and many other matters would be insignificant. Do you agree? Why?

What do you think are the reasons that those who have experienced love and forgiveness through salvation because of Christ's sacrifice would not want the richness and power of a Spirit-filled life?

I think that one reason might be lack of knowledge of the Word of God. There are many places in the Bible that talks about the relationship we Christ followers have with the Lord Jesus Christ, Father God and the Holy Spirit. Look at these verses and fill in the blanks:

1. Every Christian is a _____ of God. John 1:12
2. Every Christian has had their sins _____ and may continue to be cleansed from all _____ as they stay in _____ with Christ. 1 John 1:7
3. Every Christian is given the _____ to become _____ for Christ. Acts 1:8
4. Every Christian is given _____ gifts to _____ the body of believers, such as wisdom, knowledge, miracles, etc. 1 Corinthians 12
5. Every Christian has in her the _____ of God. Galatians 5:22-25

The Third Person of the Trinity is called the "Holy Spirit" almost 90 times in the New Testament. He is not called "holy" only because He is Holy God, but also because of His ministry. The Spirit is the Holy Spirit because He is the one who transforms believers and enables us to live a holy life.

It should be stated again at this point that to be "filled with the Spirit" does not mean that we receive more of the Holy Spirit, but that we give Him more of ourselves. As we yield our lives to Him and are filled with His presence, He has greater freedom to work in and through our lives, so that we may better glorify the Father.

God has given us a will to choose. We can choose to have as much or as little of Him that we want. We can be spiritually poor or we can be victorious believers. It is our choice daily. There are so many great promises in God's Word that we can claim. Through faith, they are ours. Like our salvation, the filling of the Holy Spirit is a gift from God. Both are received by the complete yielding of our will to Him.

God wants to use us in many unique ways. He desires us to be available for Him to use in circumstances of life. However, balance is always preferred over extremes. Let us not be full of ourselves, there will be no room for the Holy Spirit to do His work. You will know when the Holy Spirit is calling you to action. It is an inner awareness. It is a surge of strengthening assurance. And never forget it always exalts the Lord and gives all glory to God.

Don't be fearful of the Holy Spirit's work in you. The results will only benefit you and further prepare you for working God's purpose in you. Allow His work by drawing closer to the Father, studying His book and applying it to your life. Make a determination to do His will not your own. The changes that the Holy Spirit makes in your life will greatly enhance your prayer life, your Christian witness, and influence others to a closer relationship with Father God. And through all of that, you will find joy and fulfillment beyond measure!

### MORE OF HIM, LESS OF ME

Blessings!

# 28

# WORK IN PROGRESS

Look at 2 Peter 1:3-11 NIV and fill in the blanks.

3. His divine power has given us _____ we need for _____ and _____ through our _____ of Him who called us by His own glory and goodness. 4. Through these He had given us His very _____ and _____ _____, so that through them you may _____ in the divine nature and escape the corruption in the world caused by evil desires.

5. For this very reason, make every effort to add to your _____ goodness; and to goodness, _____ __

6. and to _____, self-control, and to self-control, _____, and to _____, godliness

7. and to godliness, _____ _____, and to _____ _____, love. 8. For if you possess these qualities in _____ _____, they will keep you from being ineffective and unproductive in your _____ of our Lord Jesus Christ.

9. But if anyone does not have them, he is nearsighted and blind and has forgotten that he has been _____ from his past sins.

*10. Therefore, my brothers, be all the _____ _____ to make your calling and election sure. For if you do these things, you will never _____,*

*11. and you will receive a rich _____ into the _____ _____ of our Lord and Savior Jesus Christ.*

These are just a few guidelines on developing Christian attitudes and attributes for living a life of growing and preparing for eternity with our Lord and Savior, Jesus Christ. Let's review them.

This scripture says that we have everything we need to grow in faith through what? (verse 3)

How do we acquire more knowledge of Him?

This more complete understanding of Jesus and the standards He has set before us seems to be in our best interests. If that's true, why aren't many Christians passionately seeking Him?

In verse 4, we see that He has given us His very great and precious promises. What are some of the promises that are special to you?

Why is it important to know and stand on these promises? (v. 4)

In verses 5-7, there are seven things that we should make every effort to add to our faith. List them below.

1.
2.
3.
4.
5.
6.
7.

Which of these qualities have been the most difficult for you to achieve? Circle that one and write in the space across from it how you are going to accomplish it in your life.

This is important because look what it says about it in verse 8. And it gets even worse in verse 9!

Read together verses 10 and 11.

Someone once said that the time we spend on planet Earth is our preparation for Heaven. God wants us to become more like His Son, Jesus and He has given us all the resources to do it. None of us are there yet. We are a work in progress!

Something that God has given to each one of us is potential. How we use and develop that potential is up to us. It should be our number one goal in this life here on planet earth as we prepare for our eternal home. Read Philippians 1:6 from the Amplified Bible:

*"And I am convinced and sure of this very thing, that He Who began a good work in you will continue until the day of Jesus Christ (right up to the time of His return), developing (that good work) and perfecting and bringing it to full completion in you."*

Wow! That's a promise we should grab a hold of! If He is willing to work in us until He returns to planet Earth, we should be willing too! My prayer for all of us dear sisters is that we have the desire and the passion to work with Him as He is working to perfect us.

We must remember though, that growth is sometimes a painful thing. Growth involves change and some of us don't like change! Growth also involves work and some of us can get pretty lazy in spiritual matters. Maybe this sounds harsh on my part, but I want to see us all in Heaven one day. Really, we all have a long way to go when we compare ourselves to Jesus. If we don't remember that, the enemy of our soul will gladly remind us of that daily. But keep in mind, sisters, that one day it will be worth all our efforts.

Our focus as we work out our salvation is to work toward the purpose to which God has called us. The way to progress is one step at a time. Remember the children's story of the hare and the tortoise? Let's encourage each other daily to stay on track and not to be so busy doing busy things that we take our eyes off the prize and not finish the race.

Look at Hebrews 12:1-2.

There will be times of weariness in our journey. Those are the times to remember those who have gone before you. Look for great examples in your own life and the ones in the Bible. Don't give up! The enemy wants you to.

In fact, he will do anything to trip you up. But you are on the victory track. He's already defeated!

Don't be distracted by people who want you to do anything that is not helping you reach your full potential. Keep pressing on through all obstacles. Be fruitful, not just busy. Being involved in so many things in life can entangle us to the point of exhaustion, but keep your eyes on Jesus. Pray for Him to direct your paths. He will help you keep life simple. You can probably think of some things right now that could be dropped from your agenda and not be missed.

Keep in mind the encouragement we just read found in Philippians 1:6 ". . . being confident of this very thing, that He who has begun a good work in you will complete it until the day of Jesus Christ."(NKJV) We are a work in progress.

Blessings!

# 29

# DRESS FOR SUCCESS
# Part 1

Back in the '70's, there was a number one best seller telling us how to dress for success. It became a fashion bible for people who wanted to use every means possible to make it big in their chosen profession. The basic idea of that book was to dress like you already had the top job or—"always dress like your boss."

Each day we have to choose what we are going to wear. People notice what we have on and it makes an impression on them, good or bad, fashion forward, or thrown together. Most of us strive for the former.

We also must make choices about another part of our attire—that is our attitudes and our actions. As Christ followers, our spiritual apparel is of far greater importance than our physical clothing. God has a dress code for us. You might call it the uniform of the day. Look at Colossians 3:12-14.

I counted seven virtues we need to work on as we strive to inmate Christ. They are:

C_____, K_____, H_____, G_____, P_____, F_____, and L_____.

How easy it is during a busy, stressful day to forget that we are God's representatives here on planet earth. Our job is to influence others to accept Jesus as their Lord and Savior. To those we positively influence, it brings life-changing benefits with eternal value.

We can say, "There's no way I can become all of these things!" or "This sounds like a perfect person and I am not!" And we would be right. We can't be all of these things in our own strength and we'll not reach perfection here on planet earth. The good news is that God doesn't expect that of us. What He does desire is willing hearts and minds to change as the Holy Spirit does His mighty work in and through us.

Many times we get a request to pray and after we've prayed, if we are not personally touched by the people or situation, we tend to put it out of our minds. (Unless the Lord has chosen us to continue to pray for the person/situation and continually brings it to our minds). When we read in the paper about an accident or a fire, we may feel compassion for a few moments or even a day, but again, we have no real connection with the people involved, so we tend to go on with our daily concerns. Some of us are wired to have more of a heart of compassion than others. How can the rest of us see the needs of others around us and care enough to do something to fill the need? We certainly realize that there is no way each of us can meet the needs of all those we come in contact with. I believe God wants us to see others through His eyes and give encouragement when the Holy Spirit nudges you. This will probably take some practice for most of us.

Compassion is more than just a momentary feeling of grief or pity. It's a deeper, more meaningful feeling that moves us to do something to help the people involved as though this circumstance touches our lives as well. It's loving people in the way God loves people.

According to 1 John 3: 17-18, what is the simplest test of the reality of our relationship with God?

This love of God that is in us is the reason we can show compassion. Don't wait until you feel like it to show compassion. Pray for it. If we're open to the Lord and begin to follow through on opportunities, He'll equip us with the love we need. We can count on the Holy Spirit to love others through us, (if we let Him).

Jesus was compassionate not only to the multitudes but also to the individual. He loves the world but also loves each of us personally. Mark 1:40-42 and Matthew 9:36 record two great examples of this. Read them now.

The personal touch is always the most powerful touch. Dr. Peck, a great soul winner of the last century, said that if he were given ten years in which to win 1000 souls in order to get to Heaven, he would choose to speak personally to people rather than from a pulpit. We can have more influence over the one next to us than any organization could have. Why is that true?

We all respond differently to the personal touch. Who is someone you know who have unmet physical, emotional, or spiritual needs? Can you think of at least one thing you could do to help meet one of those needs?

Let me caution here—you can't be all things to all people. God doesn't want that for us. That's His function. The fact is if you try to do what everyone asks of you, you'll have no time for yourself, your family, and most importantly for God. Some people really need our time and compassion. And some will take advantage of your generosity. Allow the Holy Spirit to guide you. Love people, but set boundaries, the Holy Spirit will guide you in this too.

AM I LIKE CHRIST?

If I am unmoved by the world sick with sin,
If I make no effort my neighbor to win,
If I'm hard and calloused to others in need,
If I've made no attempt the starving to feed,
AM I LIKE CHRIST?
If the fields, white unto harvest give no challenge to go,
If the life-bearing seed, I'm unwilling to sow,
If comfort in life is my only end,
If away from the costly I quickly tend,
AM I LIKE CHRIST?
If I am unwilling to give of my time,
If I must pause hours when giving a dime,
If I give not my utmost to see others won,
If I pray not unceasingly till life's work is done,
AM I LIKE CHRIST?
Author unknown

The next virtue we find in Colossians 3 is kindness. This should be pretty easy because kindness is one of the fruit of the Spirit and that means we Christ followers have the spirit of kindness already in us.

Does anyone have an example of a kindness done to you that you would share?

There is a good account in 2 Samuel 9:1-12 of a kindness David showed his friend, Jonathan's family. Let's look at it together.

The friendship between David and Jonathan, the son of David's mortal enemy, Saul, was powerful and loyal to the end. Just before they parted for the last time, David swore by his love to Jonathan that as long as both their houses existed, he would show kindness to Jonathan's descendants. This was a tremendous commitment because ordinarily when a king came to power, he banished all who had come before him. Many years later, David reigned over all of Israel. In the passage we just read, David's promise to his good friend is fulfilled.

What steps did David have to take to find Mephibosheth?

Put yourself in David's place. What reasons do you think David might have had for not being kind to Mephibosheth?

In what specific ways did David show kindness to Mephibosheth?

Do you have someone in your own life like this (remember we all are handicapped in some way)? As a Christian, what are some reasons we would have to show kindness to such a person in our lives?

What were the benefits to Mephibosheth and how did his life change because of David's kindness?

What are the benefits to us when we show kindness in the name of Jesus?

These are only two virtues we can clothe ourselves with to be successful in God's eyes. Compassion and kindness may come easy for you. But remember that to be dressed for success, we must also put on humility, gentleness, patience, forgiveness and love!

Chose to be fashion forward (spiritually speaking) and meet with us next time when we'll continue our study about dressing for success God's way.

**KINDNESS IS CHRISTIANITY WITH ITS WORKING CLOTHES ON!**

Blessings!

# 30

# DRESS FOR SUCCESS
# Part 2

(humility, gentleness, and patience)

Last time we talked about the importance of God's dress code for all believers. As Christ followers, we are to clothe ourselves with compassion, kindness, humility, gentleness, patience, forgiveness, and love. These are all part of daily choices we must make to dress for success in your spiritual journey.

One thing all women want when they look in the mirror is to know they look good. God desires that too when He looks at us through His own mirror. He sees what's on the inside and values our spiritual attire as being of far greater importance than our physical clothing. He wants us to take on the appearance of His Son, Jesus Christ.

Jesus talks about being humble in the Sermon on the Mount (Matthew 5-7) when He gives us a list of qualities for blessed living here on planet earth. In Matthew 5:3 He says, *"Blessed are the poor in spirit, for theirs is the kingdom of heaven."*(NKJV) Being poor in spirit sounds kind of negative, but we are truly blessed if we accept the fact that we can't make it on our own and that we need God on a daily basis.

We are blessed if we acknowledge a serious need for a deep and meaningful relationship with our Creator. We are blessed if we trust and obey God completely. He is in control of our lives and we are living out His divine plan for us. Poor in spirit is to be humble and lowly in our own eyes, not relying on our own wisdom or strength, but on God's wisdom and strength.

What quality would be the opposite of *"poor in spirit'*?

What is the promise in Matthew 5:3?

Why must a person humble herself and acknowledge spiritual need in order to enter the Kingdom of Heaven?

Sin has separated us from God. In order for us to benefit from the promise of verse 3 and enter the Kingdom of Heaven, we must first receive God's precious plan of salvation.

Look up and record John 3:16.

There may be a time in your life when someone will ask you, "How can I become a Christian?" Be prepared and you will be blessed as you lead someone to Christ. The simple plan is in these verses:

Believe … John 3:36 Repent … Acts 17:30 Confess … 1 John 1:9 Receive … John 1:12

Stop now and review these verses. If you or anyone in your group is unsure of their salvation or wish to receive this life changing gift, now is the perfect time. Pray using these verses to receive Jesus into your life.

Anyone who recognizes their spiritual need and humbly ask Jesus to be their Lord and Savior will go to heaven. So simple, but a sobering thought when you look around at your unsaved loved ones and know that you could be the one that could lead them to Jesus. Be prepared, be bold, and be blessed. Eternity hangs in the balance.

In Jesus we find the greatest example of humility. Look at Philippians 2:3-11.

If we take on this attitude of humility described in verses 3-5, how would the world react to us?

What would God's response be?

Another part of God's wardrobe is gentleness. What are some words that describe gentleness?

Is this a quality for "motherly women" or can "real men" possess this quality also?

Who is the gentlest person you know? Why?

We all have different temperaments and personalities. Some of us are naturally upbeat, some are easily angered, others tend toward depression, and others tend to be laid back. How does your particular temperament affect how you express gentleness?

Gentleness is a fruit of the Spirit, (see Galatians 5:22-23). That means that the seed of gentleness is inside of you if you are a Christ follower. Seeds must be nurtured and encouraged in order to grow. For the seed of gentleness to grow in us, we need to study it and practice it. Look at these verses to help us to grow in the area of gentleness.

Colossians 3:16

This is one reason why we need to read our Bibles, so that it can dwell in us richly. To dwell means to _____ in us. How can we teach right living to our children if we don't know God's Word? How can we encourage a sick or hurting friend if we don't have any of God's truths to share with them? How can we be the perfect helpmate to our husbands if we don't know God's instructions on marriage relationships?

What does singing psalms and spiritual songs with gratitude to God sound like to you?

Colossians 3:17

Does this verse say gentle and soothing to you or harsh and unfeeling? We need to remember that we are God's representatives here on planet Earth and honor Him through our words and deeds.

Romans 12:10-12

Did you ever hear the saying, "It's like Heaven on Earth"? Well, wouldn't this kind of unselfish devotion and gentleness in spirit be like what our relationships in Heaven will be like?

Proverbs 15:1 and Proverbs 15:4

The Spirit of gentleness that is in each of us tends to show up in our words. We need to be very careful of what comes out of our mouths. A gentle tongue can have healing power to restore and uplift those around us. It is amazing how an angry situation can change with gentle words and actions.

Name some of the things that you have no patience for.

How do you handle difficult people, (those who really bug you!) in your life?

I read a book once called, "I Prayed for Patience and Other Horror Stories." (by Chuck Snyder) It is true that when you pray for patience, God will surely answer your prayer with situations that will stretch your patience muscles. He desires for us to have this virtue because those who persevere will be blessed. Look at James 1:12.

This is one of the most powerful passages in the Bible on patience and perseverance. Do you want to be blessed? Stand firm in your trial. Do you want to be rewarded? Stand firm in that tough circumstance. Be patient—because patience really does pay off. God promises blessings and rewards to those who persevere and stand firm in hard times, but the reason we can stand firm is because He loves us unconditionally and promises to walk with us through every dark moment life will bring. Nothing touches our life that does not pass through God's hand, with His permission.

The story is told of a man who lost a job, a fortune, a wife, and a home, but he held onto his faith because it was all he had left. One day, he stopped to watch some men building a stone church. One of the workers was chiseling a triangular piece of rock. "What are you going to do with that?" asked the man. The workman said, "Do you see that little opening way up there near the spire? Well, I'm shaping this down here so that it will fit up there." Tears filled the eyes of the broken man as he walked away. It seemed that God had spoken through the workman to explain the trials of his life. God is using the trials here on earth to refine and purify us.

Patience pays off in many ways, but one of the greatest rewards of patience is joy, a deeply-rooted confidence that God is in control. And when He is in control of our life, we will have the patience to stand firm in the trials life on planet Earth brings.

Next time we will study the last two virtues in dressing for success—forgiveness and love. Are you feeling a spiritual make-over here?

Blessings!

# 31

# DRESS FOR SUCCESS
# Part 3

(forgiveness and love)

Colossians 3:12-14:

"*Therefore, as God's chosen people, holy and dearly loved, clothe yourselves with <u>compassion, kindness, humility, gentleness, and patience</u>. Bear with each other and <u>forgive</u> whatever grievances you may have against one another. <u>Forgive as the Lord forgave you</u>. And over all these virtues put on <u>love</u>, which bind them all together in perfect unity.*" NIV

God wants us to look super fine and excellent. When He looks into the mirror of our hearts, He is pleased when He can see that we are working on these virtues that are in the likeness of His Son, Jesus. What are some of the reasons that He wants this bit of excellence for us?

Today, we are studying the last two virtues, forgiveness and love. If you have been living on planet Earth for very long, someone has surely offended you in some way. Whether the offense was intentional or not, it probably left a wound. I've come to the conclusion that for our own sakes, we must forgive.

We must also forget to the extent that we can't continue to dwell on it. We can learn a lesson from the incident and move on as quickly as possible. Some offenses will take longer than others, but moving on can scab over the wound, inhabiting the offense will keep the wound festering and will never heal.

Take a few minutes here and think about an offense that has been eating away at you for some time now. (I don't mean to bring negative feelings into this study, but I promise it will get better.) Now write down the offense and how it made you feel. Next, take a moment to ask God to instill in you a generous helping of forgiveness for the person who offended you. He will answer your prayer if you are sincere. Now rip that piece of paper into tiny pieces and throw them in the trash.

Feel better? I hope so because carrying a grudge or holding onto resentment is not in our own best interests.

How are we physically affected when we choose not to forgive? See Job 21:23-25

How does unforgiveness affect our spiritual lives? Look at Mark 11:25

Job 5:2 (NIV) says that *"Resentment _____ a fool . . . ."* Why do you think this is so?

Unforgiveness robs us in so many ways. Many times we hold onto an offense while the offending person has gone on her merry way and has completely forgotten all about it. How sad it that?

Forgiveness is God's way and He shows it in an awesome manner. Forgiveness must be our choice too. Hatred and bitterness and regret are not part of God's plan for our lives. Forgiveness is.

Look at Proverbs 17: 9a and write it here:

It's a hard thing to love the person who has acted in an offensive way towards you, but not impossible—with God's help.

The last virtue we are looking at today is love. Remember what our theme verse in Colossians says about love—

*"And over all these virtues put on <u>love,</u> which bind them all together in perfect unity."* (3:14 NIV)

The love we are talking about here is called *Agape Love*. It is the kind of love we as a community of believers have for one another. It is totally unselfish love that has the capacity to give and keep on giving without expecting anything in return.

We can disagree on a subject but not carry a grudge. We can fill a need when the opportunity comes along; knowing that we can expect someday to need assistance and help will be there for us.

This Agape Love is found 225 times in the New Testament. To love one another is to seek the other's highest good. The reason we can love like this is because God first loved us. See 1 John 4:19.

Some people don't accept the fact that God loves them. In fact they don't even love themselves. But God's unfailing love is so great that all you need is a tiny seed inside you and the transforming power of the Holy Spirit's work in you can change an unloving person into a loving person. But wait—you do have a tiny seed of love inside of you if you are a believer. Love is another one of the fruit of the Spirit and the Holy Spirit has already been at work in you!

As we read the following verses, underline or circle the thoughts that are meaningful to you.

1 John 4:7-21 NKJV:

*⁷Beloved, let us love one another, for love is of God; and everyone who loves is born of God and knows God.*

*⁸ He who does not love does not know God, for God is love.*

*⁹ In this the love of God was manifested toward us, that God has sent His only begotten Son into the world, that we might live through Him.*

*¹⁰ In this is love, not that we loved God, but that He loved us and sent His Son to be the propitiation for our sins.*

*¹¹ Beloved, if God so loved us, we also ought to love one another.*

*¹² No one has seen God at any time. If we love one another, God abides in us, and His love has been perfected in us.*

*¹³ By this we know that we abide in Him, and He in us, because He has given us of His Spirit.*

*¹⁴ And we have seen and testify that the Father has sent the Son as Savior of the world.*

*¹⁵ Whoever confesses that Jesus is the Son of God, God abides in him, and he in God.*

[16] *And we have known and believed the love that God has for us. God is love, and he who abides in love abides in God, and God in him.*

[17] *Love has been perfected among us in this: that we may have boldness in the day of judgment; because as He is, so are we in this world.*

[18] *There is no fear in love; but perfect love casts out fear, because fear involves torment. But he who fears has not been made perfect in love.*

[19] *We love Him because He first loved us.*

[20] *If someone says, "I love God," and hates his brother, he is a liar; for he who does not love his brother whom he has seen, how can he love God whom he has not seen?*

[21] *And this commandment we have from Him: that he who loves God must love his brother also.*

Why is love important? (4:16-17)

How is love made complete? (16-17)

What does perfect love do? Why? (18)

Why should we love? (19)

What is the relationship between loving God and loving your brother? (20-21)

How can we demonstrate our love for others?

**Love is the hammer that breaks the hardest heart.**

We achieve success through our service to others. Sometimes we will fall short in our godly attitudes. When we clothe ourselves with compassion, kindness, humility, gentleness, patience, forgiveness and love, we are successful and lovely in God's eyes.

Begin the day by acknowledging Jesus as the Person in charge. Think of Him as your Boss, the One you desire to be like. Let His Word richly dwell in you. (Colossians 3:16) Be filled with His Spirit. (Acts 2:38) Tell of His works to all that you met. (Mark 16:20) Mediate on His Word day and night then you will be successful. (Joshua 1:8) That is the way to climb the corporate ladder in His company!

Blessings!

# 32

# DON'T PUT GOD IN A BOX

Sometimes we tend to put God in a box, (set limits on Him) when we should be putting our problems or our past or our bad habits in a box and throwing it in the trash. We forget that God is limitless. Nothing is impossible for Him. (see Mark 10:27)

A miracle is defined as something that can only happen through the divine power of God Almighty. The first miracle we should recognize is as close to us as our breath—it is the very air we breathe. Providing air for everyone on the planet is something that only God is capable of. Stop for a moment and think about how important this is to you personally—this mixture of invisible, odorless, tasteless gases (as nitrogen and oxygen) that surrounds the earth.

We see God's hand at work all the time when the nightly news reports how homes and buildings were destroyed by tornados but no lives were lost. You or someone you know might have been in a car accident and your car was totaled, but no one was seriously hurt. If we dare to say that these occasions are just coincidences, then don't expect any miracles to happen to us.

God's infinite power is beyond human understanding. There's a reason for this—He is God and we are not. But when we trust Him with everything we are and everything we have, we will experience the miraculous results of His unfailing love and unlimited power.

Biblical miracles are found in both the Old and New Testaments. Many of these miracles show God's power over nature and others show His love and mercy for those who love Him. These events are supernatural and can only be the work of God.

Moses is one example of a life of God's unlimited power. Saved as a Hebrew baby from certain death, he grew up in the palace of the king of Egypt only to, one day; lead his people out of Egypt to freedom and the Promised Land. God parts the waters of the Red Sea so that Moses and two million or more folks can walk across on dry land and escape the hands of their enemy. Later on in his life, Moses is invited to a mountain top and given a set of laws written in stone by the very hand of God. How's that for amazing, awesome, miraculous work of an unlimited God? Oh, and did I mention that Moses was so insecure in his speaking abilities that he wanted his brother to speak for him?

We can read about Moses' life and see clearly how God worked out all these things. However, Moses himself didn't have that option. He went along day by day, just as we do with no clear picture of what the future had in store for him. If God worked miraculously in the life of Moses, why would we think He would do any less for us?

Have you seen any miracles in your own life or in the life of someone you know? Share if you will.

One of my favorite stories as a child growing up in the church was Daniel and the Lion's Den. Maybe the reason we don't think of it as a miracle (God doing what only He can do) is because we're heard the story so often that we think of it as a fairy tale. But it *really* did happen. Look at the account in Daniel 6.

In verses 1-9 we learn that Daniel is highly respected, responsible and completely trustworthy. He was so highly favored by the king that there were others in high positions that were jealous and planned to have Daniel brought down. The plan was to have the king sign a law that anyone who prays to anyone, divine or human, except the king would be thrown into the den of lions. (v.7)

# AM I MY SISTER'S KEEPER?

Why do you think some people, when they see excellence in behavior, are jealous instead of inspired to do better themselves?

Read verses 10-13.

Would you have thought any less of Daniel if he had gone home to pray but just not in front of his window? Would that have mattered to God? After all Daniel would have just been protecting himself. Right?

Have you ever hidden the fact (or just not mentioned) that you are a Christ follower? What was the result?

Does the fact that the king favored Daniel have anything to do with the fact that Daniel was faithful in prayer?

For the rest of the story read verses 14-28.

King Darius didn't have a very good night. How do you think Daniel's night was?

Do you agree or disagree with the punishment of the men and their families? Why?

The account of Daniel and the lion's den is an example of God's goodness and faithfulness to a faithful and courageous follower. God could have easily stopped the whole plan before Daniel was thrown in with the lions, but He chose to save Daniel in this very creative way to show His divine power over any situation. God will not be put in a box!

Has God ever protected you from a "lion's den"? (Lion's den meaning a bad situation.)

Look up the verse below and fill in the blanks.

Zephaniah 3:17: *"The Lord your God is _____ you, He is mighty to _____. He will take great _____ in you, He will _____ you with His _____, He will _____ over you with _____."* NIV

This is one of those verses that causes us know without a doubt that our God cares about each one of us as His precious children. How awesome is that?

We all know about God's unlimited love, (John 3:16) and His unlimited comfort, (2 Corinthians 1:3-4) and His gift of grace, (Ephesians 2:8-9) and so many more of His unlimited attributes. Although we know these things and much more in our heads, it is the trusting of our hearts that make Him unlimited in our lives. Until we can trust Him with our everything, we are putting Him in a box. Free Him to be all things in your life, like this following story:

### How To Ride A Bicycle

First I saw God as my observer, my judge keeping track of the things I did wrong, so as to know whether I merited heaven or hell when I die. He was out there, sort of like the President. I recognized his picture when I saw it, but I didn't really know Him.

Later on, it seemed as though life was rather like a bike ride . . . but, it was a tandem bike, and I noticed that God was in the back letting me peddle. I don't know just when it was that He suggested to me that we change places, but life has not been the same since.

When I had control, I knew the way. It was rather boring, but predictable. It was the shortest distance between two points. But when He took the lead, He knew insightful long cuts, up mountains, and through rocky places and at breakneck speed. It was all I could do to hang on, even though it looked like madness, He said, "have faith."

Feeling worried and anxious I asked, "Where are you taking me?" He laughed and didn't answer, and I started to learn to trust.

I let go of my boring life and entered into the adventure, and when I said, "I'm scared." He'd lean back and touch my hand. He took me to people with gifts that I needed, gifts of healing, acceptance and joy. They gave me their gifts to take with me on my journey . . . our journey. God's and mine and we're off again. He said, "Give the gifts away; they're extra baggage, too much weight." So I did, to the people I met, and found that in giving, I received, and still my burden was light.

I did not trust Him at first, in control of my life, I thought He'd wrecked it, but He knows bike secrets. He knows how to make it bend to take sharp corners, jump to clear high passes, and fly through shorter scary passages.

I am learning to shut up and peddle in the strangest places, and I'm beginning to enjoy the view, and the cool breeze on my face, with God as my pure light, and as my constant source of inner power.

When I'm sure I just can't do any more, He smiles and says, "just keep peddling".
Author unknown

Does God have unlimited access in your life? Until He does you will never have a life of unlimited victory. Don't put God in a box.

Blessings!

## 33

# SEEING IS BELIEVING

Remember the old saying, "Seeing is believing"? Do you remember the beginning of your faith walk when you were so aware of God that you saw Him everywhere? I saw Him in nature, in sunsets, and in everything around me. I saw scriptures more clearly where as before this spiritual awaking I thought the Bible was pretty dull. I also saw Jesus on the faces of Christians who were willing to be used by Him and for His glory.

When I was 11 years old, I had a friend named Rosemary. She was my neighbor whose father was a pastor. She took me to church one Sunday morning and on a Sunday morning soon after that, I accepted an invitation to come forward and kneel at the altar of the church and asked Jesus to come into my heart. Share when you were first introduced to Jesus.

I'm not sure I knew what that meant and I'm not sure but what I went forward because my friends were going. At that time in my life, it was so much easier to be a follower rather than a leader.

One thing I am certain of however is that there were no New Christian classes or talk of disciplining or mentoring to teach me what was expected of me and what I could expect after I had made this decision.

Fortunately, I had parents who were committed to getting my brother, my sister, and me to Sunday school every Sunday, even though they weren't Christ followers themselves. It was there that I had the opportunity to meet and observe some Christian role models. When I got older and was a Sunday school teacher and CYC teacher myself, I often thought of what a huge responsibity it is to be a Christian role model, especially to children. It's been said that some people's only glimpse of Jesus is through you.

One thing I've learned working with children is that it's not so much what's being taught as how it's being taught. If a teacher spends the whole class time talking about Jesus' love and then is seen yelling and being impatient with her own children, the lesson of love is forgotten. Kids can spot a phony a mile away!

I remember some of my Sunday school teachers as I was growing up. They were the ones who told us stories from the Bible with joy on their faces. They were kind and interested in us. They had time for us and arranged field trips and class parties for us. And they were the ones who acted the same at a ball game or the grocery store as they did on Sunday morning. I probably didn't recognize Him at the time, but I saw Jesus in those faces.

Do you remember your first Christian role model? What was it that made them special in your eyes? Do you have that same virtue today?

All of us want this godly influence to radiate from us. We love the Lord and want to make an impact on others for Him. We have to do more than want it or wish for it. We have to make it happen. It takes time, work and commitment, but God will bless us richly for our efforts.

Look up one of my favorite verses . . . Psalm 42:1-2.

What is the difference in knowing about water and actually experiencing quenching your thirst with water?

What is the one thing that these four verses instruct us to do?

2 Chronicles 15:2
Lamentations 3:25
Deuteronomy 4:29
Matthew 6:33

# AM I MY SISTER'S KEEPER?

If we are serious about our faith and want to grow spiritually, we must be constantly seeking knowledge from the Bible and through spending time with the Lord. Many of you have small children at home. It won't hurt them at all to see your open Bible on the table or to catch you praying.

I read once about a woman who was having a hard time finding a place to pray because whenever she sat down, her children would be climbing all over her wanting her attention. She solved the problem by climbing into her children's play pen. We sisters are very resourceful!

Our pursuit of His presence will be obvious to others and our influence will be felt as a *"sweet fragrance of Christ."* (2 Corinthians 2:15AMP) But even more than that, our aggressively pursuing His presence will be pleasing to Him.

Ours is a faith-based religion. We put our hope and trust in Someone we have never physically seen and yet, the more we pursue knowledge of Him, the stronger our faith becomes.

When you think of not believing until you actually see, what Bible character comes to mind?

Read more about this disciple in John 20: 24-29.

How gracious Jesus was to reassure Thomas. I don't think he deserves the title, "Doubting Thomas." At the end of his life his faith was so strong that he died as a martyr by being speared to death.

I don't believe that God holds it against us when we question the things we don't understand. He is far more interested in our honesty and our efforts to seek the truth. After all, He made us with inquisitive and inquiring minds. We only have to offer Him our willing and trusting hearts and He will make known the issues we question. Not all of our questions may be answered this side of heaven, but I know He will honor our seeking by revealing Himself in other ways. Faith is trusting in the unseen and somewhere in our faith journey, we must let go and take that leap.

Seeing is believing—that is the influence we want to have on others. When we are serious about our faith, we want people to see Jesus in our faces, our attitudes and our actions. Being an influence for the Kingdom of God is our purpose here on planet Earth. That's the reason why God left us here after

He redeemed us. Let us praise Him for this opportunity and for the living hope we look forward to at the end of this earthly journey.

1 Peter 1:3-9: (from the New King James Version)

*³"Blessed be the God and Father of our Lord Jesus Christ, who according to His abundant mercy has begotten us again to a living hope through the resurrection of Jesus Christ from the dead, ⁴ to an inheritance incorruptible and undefiled and that does not fade away, reserved in heaven for you,*

*⁵ who are kept by the power of God through faith for salvation ready to be revealed in the last time.*

*⁶ In this you greatly rejoice, though now for a little while, if need be, you have been grieved by various trials, ⁷ that the genuineness of your faith, being much more precious than gold that perishes, though it is tested by fire, may be found to praise, honor, and glory at the revelation of Jesus Christ,*

*⁸ whom having not seen you love. Though now you do not see Him, yet believing, you rejoice with joy inexpressible and full of glory,⁹ receiving the end of your faith—the salvation of your souls."*

That, my sisters, is a lot of truth for us to digest all at once! Let's go back and as we read it again, underline the key thoughts in each verse.

As we close today, let's read these questions. You may not have the answers to them right now, but spend a little time this afternoon thinking about your responses.

1. How do you see Jesus?
2. How do you see your relationship with Him?
3. How do you see eternity?
4. Do you believe everything in the Bible?
5. If someone asks you to explain how you can believe in someone you can't see, how would you answer?

*"But in your hearts set apart Christ as Lord. Always be prepared to give an answer to everyone who asks you to give the reason for the hope that you have. But do this with gentleness and respect."* 1 Peter 3:15 NIV

Blessings!

## 34

# GLOBAL POSITIONING SYSTEM (G.P.S.)

When we go on trips we take Lola with us. She tries to keep us on track and insists that we make every turn according to her plan. When something of interest comes up during the course of our trip and we veer off course, she throws a fit and yells at us to make a "U-Turn immediately!" Right after she frantically says "recalculating, recalculating!" Sometimes we get sick of hearing her sometimes irritating and know-it-all voice and we just turn her right off. But when we decide to give her another chance, we turn her back on and all is forgiven. You might have guessed that Lola is the name of our GPS.

Lola has many fine and helpful qualities and has helped us arrive many times at the right destination, but she's a little single-minded. Sometimes we just want to be foot-loose and fancy-free. While that may be fun for a vacation, most of our life should have a good plan and direction.

*"Do not turn to the right or the left. Remove your foot from evil."*
Proverbs 4:27NKJV

Fortunately God does have a plan and has installed a GPS inside all those who believe in and are committed to His Son. Not only that, but His Book is a compass to show us the right path to take. Psalm 119:105 says: *"Your word is a lamp to my feet and a light to my path."* (NKJV) Maps always need updating and map-quest is sometimes confusing, but *"For the word of the Lord is right and all His work is done in truth."*(Psalm 33:4) NKJV

The importance of attentiveness to God's guidance is the point of this story about the great missionary, Dr. E. Stanley Jones:

Dr. Jones spent two weeks each year traveling from city to city in India to raise funds for his mission. He scheduled three talks each day to prominent citizens in an attempt to gain their financial support. He would address one group at breakfast, a second at lunch and a third at dinner. The next day he would repeat his appeals to three groups in another city.

One night after his third presentation he rushed to the airport where he had booked the last flight of the day to his next day's destination. As he stood in line to get his seat assignment they announced that his flight was oversold and requested that passengers give up their seats in return for an additional free round-trip ticket to the city of their choice.

When the agent had finished his announcement, Jones thought he heard the Lord whisper to him, "Step out of the line." He hesitated. If he didn't take this flight he would miss at least two of his meetings the next day—and the money he hoped to raise. He stayed in line.

When he was nearly to the podium he again felt God urging him to step out of line and give up his seat. Again he hesitated, not sure if it was God speaking to him, or only his imagination. But when he was just one person away from the airline agent, he again heard God speak, this time in no uncertain terms: "Step out of the line!" Jones obeyed and someone else took his place.

That airliner crashed and all aboard were killed. When the media learned that Dr. Jones had not been aboard as scheduled, they rushed to interview him. When told why he had not been aboard the ill-fated flight they were incensed. "Do you mean to tell us that you were the only one God loved enough to warn?" they asked incredulously.

"Oh no!" came Jones's quick reply. "I don't mean that at all! I know God loved every person aboard that plane at least as much as He loves me. But, you see, I was the only one who was listening."(source unknown)

Haven't we all heard that still, small voice and wondered "is that really You, God?" Maybe He's whispering something we don't want to hear. Maybe it doesn't fit into our plans right now. The problem with ignoring that voice is that after a while He won't bother you anymore.

How often do we pray for God's guidance and then go on about the busyness of life not giving another thought to the answer God is trying to reveal to us? Or another instance might be that as we are praying about a situation, we explain just what we think should happen to resolve the problem, not even thinking it is possible that He has another better solution—since after all—He is God.

God Has given us two ears and one mouth for a reason!

The first step in knowing God's plan for our lives is to develop a close, personal relationship with His Son, Jesus Christ. And then to continue to grow and mature in Christ-likeness as you apply the principles found in God's word. Another sure expectation is that God has work for each one of us to accomplish—something that is uniquely fitted for you alone.

Look at Ephesians 2:10:

*"For we are His workmanship, created in Christ Jesus for good works, which God prepared beforehand that we should walk in them."* NKJV

This verse seems to be saying that God is first working in us to prepare us for the particular tasks He will assign to us when we are ready to do the work. Do you agree?

Describe your feelings when you read you are God's workmanship. Other translations use the words God's handiwork or God's masterpiece. Is this how you look at yourself? Explain.

God has given us many resources to prepare ourselves for the tasks He has designed for us to do. Resources like seeds of each of the Fruit of the Spirit, unlimited communication with Him, at least one spiritual gift, great examples of those who have gone on before us and an unending supply of love, encouragement, wisdom and hope through His Word. Oh, and one more thing—the precious blood of Jesus as a covering.

Just think what a difference we could make if we would only use all of these resources available to us. It is foolishness to go through life without a clue about our purpose or direction. God will ask us two questions when we stand before Him one day. The first is . . . "What did you do with My Son?" (Did you accept what Jesus did for you on the cross and did you learn to love and trust Him?) And the second is . . . "What did you do with what I gave you?" (What did you do with your life? Did you use your time, treasure and talents on yourself or did you live to help others and glorify Me?) It should be our goal in life to be able to give Him a positive answer when that time comes.

**The way to heaven . . . turn right and go straight!**

Each of these verses will give us understanding in what God desires of us. Share your thoughts after we look at each one:

~James 2:14-18
How can you handle a person who says he is a Christian, but doesn't act like one?

Do you know someone who is good and kind to everyone, but you know she doesn't have the Lord in her life? What can you do to convince her to say "yes" to Jesus?

~Ephesians 5:15-17
We all know time is short on planet Earth but how can we recognize an opportunity when it comes along?

What if we feel that we're not in the right place at the right time to seize an opportunity?

How can we understand what the Lord's will is?

~Proverbs 3:1-6
These verses list some benefits of godly wisdom. List all that you can find.

Which of these benefits mean the most to you?

God is our provider. He provides us with resources and the freedom to choose to use them or not. What are some indications that you are on the right path for your life?

Jeremiah 29: 11 says that God has a plan for our lives. To follow that plan we must know what in peculiar He has called us to do. Here are some questions to help us be sure that we've heard Him correctly:

Is it consistent with the Word of God?
Is it a wise decision?
Can I honestly ask the Lord to help me achieve this?
Do I have genuine peace about it?
Does this decision fit who I am as a follower of Jesus?
Does it fit the Lord's overall plan for my life?
Will this decision honor God?

*"A man's heart plans his way, but the Lord directs his steps."* Proverbs 16:9NKJV

Blessings!

# 35

# WHEN UPSIDE DOWN MAKES SENSE

The Bible says that God's thoughts are higher than our thoughts. Sometimes we see Him working and we are sure that we have a better way. But then the end result of the situation turns out better than we could ever hope or imagine and it's settled in our minds-yes, God does work all things out for our good in ways that don't seem to make sense to us at the time.

For instance, if you were God, wouldn't you have sent your son as a king and not a little baby? And having Him born in a stable where animals are fed and kept, does that make sense to you? And here are some other mysteries:

The greatest Man in history, Jesus, had no servants, yet they called Him Master. Jesus had no degree, yet they called Him Teacher. He had no medicines or medical license, but they called Him Healer. He had no army, yet kings feared Him. He won no military battles, yet Jesus conquered the world.

Jesus committed no crime, yet they crucified Him. He was buried in a tomb, yet He lives today. Wow! Pretty amazing!

Besides creating us and giving us a whole world to live in and free choice and sending His Son to die in our place, God also wrote a Book for us. This is where we can find many of the answers to the things that don't make sense. Look at John 3:16-17 and that will tell you why Jesus came from Heaven to this world we live in. If you had to explain the reason why He came in one word, what would it be?

In God's way of doing things, there's a lot that doesn't make sense to us. Let's look at some of them in the Bible.
Matthew 20:26-28 talks about greatness is becoming a servant. Read the verses together and share your thoughts.

Those who desire to be great, usually have a pretty big ego. How does this attitude not work for growing, committed Christ-followers?

Is there any task too small or humbling for a Christian? Think of an example in Jesus' life.

Name some people who have achieved greatness, but have a humble spirit.

This upside down principle of being a servant to become great works in our every day circumstances too. People have respect for someone with a modest, unassuming spirit and their influence can carry a lot of weight while someone who is full of themselves is not respected. And even worse, they can't be used by God.

When you're full of yourself, God can't fill you. But when you empty yourself, God has a useful vessel.

Luke 6:38 *"Give, and it will be given to you. A good measure, pressed down, shaken together and running over, will be poured into your lap. For with the measure you use, it will be measured to you."* NIV

Remember Y2K, when people brought extra supplies and hoarded all kinds of things? What would the world be like if that happened all the time? What makes a generous spirit?

This verse in Luke is good counsel from our Heavenly Father. Go back and read it again. Have you tested this principle?

Think of a time when God generously gave you something unexpected. Explain.

Is generosity contagious? Why or why not?

2 Corinthians 12:9 *"And He said to me, "My grace is sufficient for you, for My strength is made perfect in weakness." Therefore most gladly I will rather boast in my infirmities, that the power of Christ may rest upon me."* NKJV

In the previous verses, Paul is asking the Lord to take away the thorn in his flesh. We don't really know what it was, but instead of granting his request, the Lord gave him grace instead. What is grace?

Look at 2 Corinthians 9:6-11. What are some of the things that we are to do and what will God do as a result of our generosity?

As Christians, our blessings are too numerous to count. It is only fitting then that we should show a generous nature to the world. Spread a little kindness where ever you go and you will be honoring God and the blessings He brings to you because of this act of service, will be immeasurable.

Why do you think that God gives only a sufficient amount of grace and not a lot of grace?

The Bible says *"when I am weak, then I am strong."* (2 Corinthians 12:10 NKJV) How does that work?

James 4:10 *"Humble yourself in the sight of the Lord and He will lift you up."* (NKJV)

In what ways can we humble ourselves before the Lord?
Are any of these things harder for you to do than others?
What can we learn from these next few verses on humility?

Luke 14:11
1 Peter 5:5
Psalm 138:6

1 Corinthians 1:27-29 *"But God has chosen the foolish things of the world to put to shame the wise, and God has chosen the weak things of the world to put to shame the things which are mighty; ²⁸ and the base things of the world and the*

*things which are despised God has chosen, and the things which are not, to bring to nothing the things that are, $^{29}$ that no flesh should glory in His presence."* NKJV

In what ways can the gospel seem foolish?

In what ways is God's wisdom different from the world's wisdom?

What does it mean when the scripture says, "God chose the weak things of the world"?

What are Christ followers suppose to brag about?

Have you sought God's guidance, rather than relying on your own wisdom and ability? Explain. Look at Proverbs 3:5-8

How can God use us, imperfect as we are?

Because God has chosen to reveal Himself in ways that seem foolish to the world, we can be a part of that revelation. Many times God uses us in ways we think as unimportant or even foolish. For example, we humans are weak, but with the Holy Spirit living and working in us, we are made strong.

God takes the humble and lifts them up. Mother Theresa was a very humble person, yet she was known all over the world for the work she did with the poor people in Calcutta. I imagine it was very hard to say "no" to her when she needed something to continue her work.

How many of us have been discouraged and turned to the Bible and soon are encouraged by the words on the pages? God's word is a never ending source of power and strength. Victory comes through defeat and healing comes through brokenness.

All of these things are the upside down principles God uses to encourage His people and to further His kingdom. They may not make sense to us, that's because they are beyond our understanding. If we knew and could understand everything God did, He would not be God to us. The good news is, we don't have to figure Him out, we just have to believe and trust. Our hope must lie in Him, because He is our only Hope.

Blessings!

# 36

# ME . . . A CLOSER LOOK ☺

We are sisters in the sisterhood of the fellowship. We sisters are a unique group of individuals who make up this assemblage. We are wonderfully and fearfully made and are treasured by our Creator. As individuals, we tend to be hard on ourselves, but able to overlook the flaws of others. We are quick to sympathize with those who are hurting and want to fix boo boos.

We love clean and don't like messy. If we have children, we want them well behaved especially in church and other public places. We tend to be loving creatures and our grandchildren can do no wrong. God gave us the role of encouragers and peacemakers, although sometimes we would just like to give someone a piece of our minds!

We are good at relationships and as sisters in the sisterhood, we have our own language that involves not finishing our own sentences because the sister we are having a conversation with already knows what we are going to say . . . and is waiting for her turn to talk.

When God made us, He included all of these qualities and more so we could succeed in the role of being "me." The most important quality He gave us was the desire to know Him. Because we are eternal beings, our home is not here on planet Earth, but Heaven and the journey we are on has Heaven as its goal.

Because God created us to be spiritual beings, He has provided us to receive many awesome blessings. Before we can claim these spiritual blessings as our own, we have to learn what they are. Today we'll be studying in the book of Ephesians. As we look at this scripture, let's fill in the blanks with the descriptions of who God thinks we are as true believers in His Son, Jesus Christ. They are powerful words for us to claim that will bring us strength and encouragement.

Ephesians 1:3—I am blessed with all _____ in Heavenly places in Christ.

What are some spiritual blessings that we have through Christ?

Ephesians 1:4—I am _____ by You, my Father, to be _____ and without _____.

Ephesians 1:5—I am Your _____ according to the good pleasure of Your will.

Parents of adopted children tell them that they are special because they were "chosen." Do you feel special because you were adopted into God's family? My husband was adopted when he was two years old. Growing up he had three brothers. They were raised by parents who chose them and gave them a good, loving home. I for one am glad they did!

Let's take a closer look at the reality of what God has done and will do in our lives:

Ephesians 1:6—He freely gives me _____ through Jesus Christ.

Ephesians 1:7—I am _____ through the blood of Jesus.

This should be number one on our praise list . . . that we have been redeemed!

Ephesians 1:8—I am a person of _____ and _____.

Ephesians 1:13—I have heard the gospel (good news) and have received _____.

# AM I MY SISTER'S KEEPER?

Ephesians 1:13—I have been marked with a _____, the promised Holy Spirit.

In what way is the Holy Spirit God's mark of ownership on us?

I've read that we only use about 10% of the brain power available to us. How about the Holy Spirit's power in our lives? How much of His power do you think you use? Are you satisfied with that?

Ephesians 1:14—I have an _____ waiting for me in heaven.

Ephesians 1:17—I have a spirit of _____ and _____ in the knowledge of Christ Jesus.

Paul prayed for the Ephesians to have a spirit of wisdom and revelation to know God better. Describe the process of knowing God better.

Ephesians 2:5—I am saved by Your _____.

### "God's Riches At Christ's Expense"

Ephesians 2:6—I am seated in _____ _____ in Christ Jesus.

Ephesians 2:10—I am Your _____.

I am encouraged by the fact that I am God's handiwork and that He will continue to work on me until the day Jesus returns. I am not perfect and I don't expect to be until I arrive in heaven. But if I continue to be willing to do His will and make His desires my desires, then I'll be on the right path. He knows I am a work in progress!

Ephesians 2:13—I am near to You by the _____ of Christ.

Ephesians 2:18—I have access to the _____.

Ephesians 2:19—I am a member of God's _____.

Ephesians 3:16—I am strengthened with _____ by Your Holy Spirit.

Ephesians 3:17—I am rooted and _____ in love.

How would you describe God's love to someone who doesn't know Him?

Ephesians 4:15—I speak the _____ in love.

God's Word is our standard of truth. The more we study it, the more truth we will know. This will change our thinking and our actions for our benefit and God's glory.

Ephesians 4:23—I am _____ in the spirit of my mind.

One of the first changes we see in a new believer is their new attitude. Our attitudes begin in our minds. The more we read and study God's word, the more our attitudes will change in a positive way.

I believe that the seed of God's love is the first and most important element that will change our attitude and then all of the other fruit of the Spirit will follow. A positive mind-set belongs to the one who is nurturing all of the seeds that God put in us when He sealed us up with the Holy Spirit.

Ephesians 5:1—I am an _____ of God and dearly loved.

Ephesians 5:2—I walk in _____.

Ephesians 5:8—I am _____ in You.

The difference between darkness and light is how clearly we can see. Our time on planet Earth is short and I don't want to spend it in a fog. The Bible teaches that for us to be free, we must know the truth. As you prepare to study God's Word, ask the Holy Spirit to reveal truth to you. We've all read passages of scripture and didn't have a clue what they meant. Asking the Holy Spirit to make clear to you what you are reading and what it means for you personally is the best way to bring light to God's Word for you.

Ephesians 5:18—I am _____ with the Holy Spirit.

Our Heavenly Father has a plan and purpose for each one of us, dear sisters. It is a unique purpose that can only be accomplished by the "me" that we are with God's help! (2:10)

I know we've looked up a lot of verses in this study but think of this: God is pleased when He hears the pages turning in His Book!

Blessings!

## 37

# GOD 101

What is usually the first thing that comes to your mind when you think about God?

A while ago, in Sunday School class, the question was asked, "When you think of God, do you think of Him as Father, Jesus and Holy Spirit, separate, or do you think of Him as One?" How would you answer this question?

The God-head has 3 parts. They are the Father, the Son, and the Holy Spirit. This 3 in 1 is called the God-head or the Trinity. Name some functions of each one.

Father God:

Jesus:

Holy Spirit:

This 3 in 1 concept shouldn't throw us at all. There are many common, every day things that are in that category:

The apple—peeling, fruit and seeds. Three parts make one apple. The egg—shell, white and yoke. Three parts make one egg.

We Sisters—body, soul, and spirit. Three parts make one sister! Our soul also has three parts—mind, will, and emotions.

There are several places in the New Testament that the Father, Son and Spirit are mentioned in the same verse or verses.

Look at Luke 3:21-22. Also take a look at 2 Corinthians 13:14.

Gracious and loving are just some of God's attributes. Write down five more of His attributes:

There are many ways to learn about God. One way is through His Word. Some call it the Handbook of Life or God's Love Letter to us, but the fact is that the Bible is the greatest book on planet Earth. It was given to us by God, so that we could know Him and is meant to be read in small amounts every day. It is a wonderful goal to read the whole Bible in a year and we all should do that, but smaller amounts at one sitting are easier for our minds to digest and process.

There are so many revelations of God in His Word. The Bible tells of His greatness, glory, honor, and character. We know that Jesus Christ is the same yesterday, today, and forever (Heb 13:8), that God's grace is sufficient for every repentant heart, and that His power is made perfect in our weakness (2 Corinthians 12:9). We know that His name is above all other names (Philippians 2:9), that there is no other like Him (Jeremiah 10:6), and that His wisdom holds secrets that are hidden from before time began (I Corinthians 2:7).

Knowing about God and knowing God personally is essential for successful living here on planet Earth. Remember where you were and what you were feeling on 9/11? Of course you do. I remember being very thankful that I knew God and felt very assured that He was in control.

But lots of people all around the country were in a panic mode. The people who didn't have a personal relationship with God stumbled around with no sense of direction and fearful of the future. Not that we Christ followers have it all together and don't fear anything, we aren't superhuman, but thank God we know that He is in control and through Him our future is secure.

What exactly is it that we are supposed to know about God? As we study more about His attributes, we will see things we can know and will help us to develop a closer, more intimate relationship with Him.

1. **God is Sovereign.** The word sovereign means chief, highest, or supreme. God is the one and only and there is no other. He is the number one ruler in the universe. In fact He insists on being number one. (refer to Exodus 20:3) When He is number one in our lives, it gives us a calm assurance that there is nothing that He doesn't know about and nothing surprises Him.

   Even 9/11 was no surprise to Him. I know many innocent people lost their lives, however reports show that many people who worked in the twin towers didn't go to work that day or were late to work for some reason. His purposes and plans rule.

Look at Psalm 103:19, Romans 9:20-21 to learn more about God's sovereignty.

Why is it important to our spiritual walk to know without a doubt that God is sovereign?

2. **God is Eternal.** The first four words of the Bible says, *"In the beginning God . . ."* There has never been a time when God did not exist. He has no beginning or end. The measure of time is man's invention and for our convenience not His. God has no boundaries in time or space or anything else.

   Knowing this about God, there is no reason not to trust Him with our lives. Picture God in an airplane high above us as we are driving down the road. He can see what we've already passed and He can see what is ahead of us. He knows what is best for us because He sees the big picture.

   Look at 1 Timothy 1:17 and Revelation 1:8. How does it help your faith to know that God always was and is and is to be? Explain.

3. **God is Omniscient.** God's knowledge is eternal and unlimited. He knows everything. He never learns nor is He ever informed by mankind. He knows when I sit and when I rise. He knows my every thought and knows what I'm going to say before the words come out of my mouth. Don't you wish sometimes we had that talent?

   God knows all there is to know about us. The knowledge of our past or future does not influence His present response to us one bit. God always deals with us on the basis of our honesty. Nothing we think or do is hidden from Him. Knowing all about us, He still forgave our sins and accepted us into His family.

Look at Isaiah 40:12-14, Hebrews 4:13 and 1 John 3:19-20 for more insight. How does the knowledge that God knows all things affect your daily walk with Him?

4. **God is Omnipresent.** God's presence is universal. He is everywhere at once. And there is nowhere that we can go that God is not there with us. Isn't that good to know? The Old Testament prophet, Jonah, found that out the hard way. Since we know that He is everywhere, it is foolish to think we can hide from Him. He has promised to never leave us or forsake us. There are times when we think He has forgotten us and there are other times when we can physically feel His very presence. The only difference in those two situations is within us.

Look at Isaiah 66:1, Jeremiah 23:24 and Acts 17:24-27. Have you ever tried to hide from God? Explain. Have you ever felt God's presence? Explain.

5. **God is Omnipotent.** God is all-powerful, nothing is impossible for Him. (Luke 1:37) His power has no limits. (Psalm 147:5) Because He is all-powerful, He can keep us, as Christ followers, from all harm and danger. (Jude 24) Our salvation is the result of the power of God. (Romans 1:16) His omnipotence is seen in His power to create. (Genesis 1:1)

Look at Ephesians 3:20 and Philippians 3:20-21. Have you learned to lean on His power and strength?

What does Philippians 4:13 mean to you?

6. **God is Immutable.** He never changes. Hebrews 13:8 tells us that *"Jesus Christ is the same yesterday, today and forever."* God never changes in His nature or His attributes. The Bible contains thousands of things that God has promised to do for those who belong to Him. He can be trusted to keep His Word. We must learn to trust Him because He is a Promise Keeper.

> Look at Proverbs 3:5-6, and James 1:17 Name some promises that are special to you. How have they impacted your life?

The attributes we studied today are non-transferrable, meaning only God has these characteristics. It is important for us to know that God is sovereign and all-powerful and omnipresent because we need Someone bigger than us to put our trust in.

Next time we'll talk about God's transferrable attributes. These are the ones we need to work on in if we are to become more like Him. Characteristics like love and patience and holiness. These are the qualities that bring great value to our daily lives here on planet Earth because we can be of so much more use to God in bringing His plans and purposes to fulfillment.

This knowledge also impacts our lives personally as we find ourselves drawn closer to the One who created us because He wants a personal relationship with us. An intimate walk with our Lord is a blessed life indeed.

Blessings!

## OUR HEAVENLY FATHER

What are different words that we use to describe our Heavenly Father? Unscramble the letters to discover various words we commonly use.

1. LYHO _____
2. NKDI _____
3. OKRC _____
4. HYGMIT _____
5. JTISMACE _____
6. OARCIGUS _____
7. UWEPROFL _____
8. EEEERRMD _____
9. GRIVEOFGN _____
10. VRELDIERE _____
11. WLOUNFDRE _____
12. GUESTHOIR _____
13. HUWORTSTYTR _____
14. STROCESAMIANO _____
15. TUGNNSADNIRED _____

Answers in the back of the book

# 38

# GOD 102

Have you ever wondered what it must have been like to be Adam and Eve in the garden, as they were walking with God in the cool of the day? (Pre-serpent days, of course!) Just picture this in your minds—a beautiful garden of every kind of flora and fauna you can imagine, the perfect temperature, not too cool and not too hot, no worries about your wardrobe, a refreshing breeze blowing the fragrance of exotic flowers your way and the most exciting ingredient in this fantasy scenario is the company you are keeping—the God of the Universe!

Is it hard for you to imagine that the Creator the whole universe wants your company? It is His heart's desire that you and He have a close relationship. In fact, that is the reason He created you in the first place. Not only that but He also wants you to know His Son personally. If you don't believe me, you can just look it up in the book He wrote for you.

Last time we talked about many of God's non-transferable attributes like His being sovereign, omnipresent and all-powerful to name a few. Knowing those things about Him cause us to worship Him for who He is. There is no other who is worthy of our praise. It also makes us want to turn over to Him the things that we know we can't handle on our own. (We know because we've already tried!) Things that make our blood pressure rise to numbers that doctors warn us about. For instance, the difficult people in our lives or the situations we have no clue how to fix or the health problems that may seem overwhelming and all the other negative, worrisome things we encounter here on planet Earth.

Having the God of the Universe on our side is a good thing. But because of busyness or laziness on our part, we don't seek to know Him as intimately as we could or should. Therefore the potential for a more peaceful, powerful, satisfying life is limited. Getting to know Him more is the purpose of this study.

The following are some of God's transferrable attributes. These attributes are the ones we strive to achieve in our lives if we want to be more like Jesus.

1. **God is patient.** How many of us have prayed for patience over the years? Just this summer when the guys were working on my house, I found many ways to perfect this virtue. Let's just say sweeping up sawdust and not being able to find my things doesn't make for a restful summer.

   But thank God that He is patient! Throughout the Bible God reveals a loving patience that shows His divine mercy. We need to continually work on this virtue. Proverbs tell us that to be patient is to be wise.

Look at Psalm 103:8, 1Timothy 1:16 and 2 Peter 3: 9 for further insights on God's patience.

Do you have an experience in learning patience that you can share? How did it change your situation?

What do the letters PBPWMGNFWMY stand for? P_____ B__ P_____ W____ M_ G_____ N____ F_____ W_____ M__ Y_____. How does knowing this give you hope? Look at Philippians 1:6.

2. **God is just.** Have you caught yourself criticizing another sister's actions? There is a Biblical principle that states: *"For judgment is without mercy to the one who has shown no mercy. Mercy triumphs over judgment!"* (James 2:13 NKJV) Another principle found in Luke 6:37 says to *"judge not, and you shall not be judged"*. (NKJV) Judging

others even in little things is not our right, only God's because He is the only one who sees the heart. That's one good reason not to judge.

Look at 1 Corinthians 4:5 and 2 Timothy 4:8 for more meaningful teaching.

Have you ever thought that life was unfair? Does it bother you when you know someone has gotten away with something?

3. **God is love.** God is perfect, limitless, for all time, unconditional love. Because of His love for us, we are able to forgive wrongs done to us and love the one who was responsible for the wrong that was done. God's love is given freely with no thought to the unloveliness or the merit of the person.

    As perfect as God's love is, however, we will never be satisfied if we just receive it and not return it. To be complete, love must flow in both directions. It must be received and returned. One of the ways to show God that you love Him is to have an attitude of gratitude. Just as we expect our children to thank us for the things we give them and do for them, our Father God wants us to give Him thanks.

Look at Zephaniah 3:17, Romans 8:38-39 and Matthew 22:37-40.

What are some other ways we can show love to God and to those around us?

Look at 1 Corinthians 13:4-7 for a definition of love from God Himself. What does He say love is? What is love not?

4. **God is truth.** He is absolute truth. There doesn't seem to be many absolutes in the world today. Truth is only truth until the lie is exposed. In recent times, many untruths have been revealed about our top government officials and those at the top of big corporations. Many promises are broken, even among the household of faith. People can put such a spin on their actions that it seems to justify their sins, in their own minds, anyway.

    I fear for those who are mocking God in this way. His Word says that *"For there is nothing hidden which will not be revealed, nor has anything been kept secret but that it should come to light."* (Mark 4:22 NKJV)

Truth is God's way. He commands His children to live in truth, and He rewards those who follow His commandments.

In a world in which the integrity of a person is often challenged, don't compromise your values. Read Romans 12:1-2 to learn what God believes we need to do to raise the standards that we live by. Write it here:

When we know the truth found in God's Word, we will not give in to the temptation to compromise our beliefs.

Look at John 8:31-32, John 1:14 and Titus 1:2 for greater insight on truth. The Bible is the standard of truth by which we should evaluate what is truth and what is false.

How could you handle a situation where someone asks you to lie? What if it meant your job? Or your relationship with someone?

5. **God is holy.** God is perfectly holy and righteous. It is impossible for Him to do or to cause anything that is wrong. All holiness begins with God. It is His fundamental nature to be holy. The word holy means to set apart from what is temporal or impure. God's holiness is linked with righteousness. As obedient children, we are to be holy because He is holy. (1Peter 1:14-16) However, we can't be holy within ourselves, but we must rely on His power and grace. (Romans 12:1-2 and Hebrews 12:11-11)

Look at Revelation 4:8 for brief look at the holiness in Heaven.

Describe what holiness looks like in Christ followers. Think of a person you know who possesses this holiness quality. What are the things you admire about this person?

6. **God is authority**. God is the sovereign authority of the universe. None of us would disagree with that statement. However, we might not agree that we, as Christ followers, also have authority as well. Colossians 2:9-10 says that we who are in Christ *"have been given fullness in Christ, who is the head over every power and authority"* (NIV) We now have His power and authority over Satan (Colossians 2:13-15) and His power and authority to impact other people. (Matthew 28:18-20)

Look at Acts 1:8 and John 14:12.

According to 2 Timothy 1:7, God has given us not a spirit of timidity but a spirit of *"power, love and discipline"*. Why aren't most believers bold and confident in their witness to the world?

Getting to know God is the most important goal we have in the short time we'll spend on planet Earth. The spirit and the genuine effort in which we seek Him, determines our life now and for all eternity.

* Please be patient with me, God's not finished with me yet.

Blessings!

## 39

# FAVOR ADDS FLAVOR

Think of this—God's many blessings in your life have increased the positive side of your everyday existence here on planet Earth. How? You ask. Here's an example—What if you were born without the ability to smile? The facial muscles needed to bring up the corners of your mouth were too weak to function correctly or didn't exist at all. A smile is just a simple thing that we take for granted, but what if no one in the world smiled? How would we express our pleasure? I believe that all of us can smile because when we came into this world, God showed favor on us and gave us smile-ability. Let's test that theory... SMILE!

Here are some other things to think about: What if God made this beautiful world we live in black and white instead of the color all around us? What if there was no music or birds singing or a host of other enjoyable things? Here's a horrible thought—what if there was no chocolate?

We can all agree that God has blessed us in many ways. Can we also agree that we take these blessings for granted and not thank Him enough?

Favor is described as good will, kindness, a yielding to another, to show partiality to, or give advantage. The frequently quoted definition of grace is

God's unmerited favor. So when we read about favor in the Bible, we can also describe it as grace.

There are many beautiful examples of God's favor in His Word. The one that comes to mind first is the Old Testament Prophet, Daniel. When Daniel was a teenager, he and many of his friends and countrymen were taken hostage by the Babylonians and taken 800 or so miles away from their own country. I know that doesn't sound like anything favorable to us, but the Hebrews could have just as easily been killed by their enemies.

It's interesting how God uses awful situations for His glory. And He did in this circumstance also. Even though Daniel and his friends were forced to be somewhere they didn't want to be, they were still committed to obedience to their God and because of their faithfulness, He was able to use them in great and powerful ways.

It was King Nebuchadnezzar's plan to train these young men to become his attendants in his court by conforming them to the customs of his country. Many of these customs were completely opposite of God's laws governing the Jewish people. Daniel and his friends could have chosen the easiest route and went along with the king's plan but had the courage to choose to remain faithful in their commitment to God.

Many of Daniel's countrymen did chose to conform to the easier way and go along with the new lifestyle. We don't read too much more about them. It must be that's the end of their story.

From the very beginning of their capture (found in Daniel 1) Daniel and his friends were polite and respectful but unwavering in their desire to obey God. It was a big deal to abide by the dietary laws their ancestors had lived by for centuries. God honored their obedience by showing favor to them in this foreign country.

It's pretty obvious, isn't it, that Daniel had a relationship with God? Daniel knew that God was in control. Because of that knowledge, he was strong enough to stand up to the king when most of the others caved under the pressure.

Read Daniel's words in chapter 11:32.

Have you ever thought about what you would do if you were called on to recant your faith in the face of torture or even death?

God strengthens and secures His people when they face challenges. You probably have already experienced this more than once. When God knows your heart is committed to Him, He will strongly support you in trouble. That's called favor. For further insight in God's support of His people see 2 Chronicles 16:9a.

Daniel's commitment to God and God's favor over him are the factors that made Daniel a victor as he spent the night in the lion's den and allowed his friends to survive the fiery furnace. These and other amazing accounts are found in the first six chapters of Daniel.

Although there are many examples of God's favor in the Bible, this divine kindness is available to us today. Look at Proverbs 3:1-4.

There are several lessons for us in these few verses. In verse 1, it says to *"keep these commands"* or *"store up these commands"* in your heart. This means not only to memorize them, but to apply them to every day living. We in the western world consider the heart as being our core or innermost being, so the things we store or keep there are the most important things to us. And not just for safe keeping, but for doing in our every life as well.

In verse 2 it states that if we keep God's commands, we will receive 2 things. What are they? _____ and _____. Living a good and long life may simply come from the wisdom of following God's laws. After all, they are given to us for our well being. The bottom line is that all things, including the length of our days, are in God's hands. I'm glad I don't have His job!

In verse 3, what does *"bind them around your neck"* and *"write them on the tablet of your heart."*

And finally in verse 4, what are the 2 promises there? _____ - _____ and _____.

Look at Luke 2:52 to see Jesus' example.

Many Bible scholars have speculated over the years about what Jesus was doing from the time He was 12 years old and was found conversing with the priests in the synagogue to the time He started His public ministry at age 30. This is what He was doing—growing in wisdom and stature and in favor with God and men. Growing takes a while. Longer for some of us than others! What kind of kid do you think Jesus was? How about as a teenager?

What does favor with God and man do to your life? (see title of study) _____!

Define flavor:

Look at Nehemiah 1:5-6. The lesson for us here is to ask God for favor especially when we are facing a difficult situation. It is a wise thing when we seek the favor of God. It is the most important relationship we are privileged to have and keeping the vertical lines of communication open is our responsibility. What is one of the ways those lines of communication is broken? _____

Look at Proverbs 14:9. What are we called if we don't take our relationship with God seriously? F _____ s God is interested in a repentant heart. Unconfessed sin leads to a separation between us and God. For us to be reconciled with Him and be able to enjoy His presence in our lives, we must first humble ourselves and simply ask. What is another word for goodwill? _____ God gives His favor to the one who has a changed heart.

What if someone ask you for a favor. Would you be more willing to grant a favor to a stranger or to someone you are close to? Of course, we would say the person we are close to. God is that way too. As we read earlier in 2 Chronicles 16:9: *"The eyes of the Lord search the whole earth in order to strengthen those whose hearts are fully committed to Him."* (NLT) How great is that!

There's a true story of a man named, Isidore Zimmerman who served 25 years in prison for a crime he didn't commit. Because of false testimony at his trial, he was convicted of killing a New York policeman. In time, however, his innocence was proven, and in 1962 he was released. But did he "live happily ever after"? No.

Even though he had been innocent all along, Zimmerman couldn't escape the stigma of being an ex-convict. What few jobs he could get soon ended when employers learned that he had served time. His record was cleared, but society did not fully accept him.

In God economy, once our sins are forgiven, God remembers them no more. To Him they are as far as the east is from the west and we are accepted into His family. Through God's mercy and favor to us, we who ask, are made righteous because of the shed blood of our Savior, Jesus Christ.

*"... so that as sin reigned in death, even so grace might reign through righteousness to eternal life through Jesus Christ our Lord."* (Romans 5:21NKJV)

This is the ultimate favor that God bestows upon us—that He gave His Son that we might have eternal life. And as children of God, we can reap the blessings that God had promised to all those who live according to His will and His word. Reaping those blessings add flavor (spice, essence, and sweet aroma) to our lives.

If you don't know Christ as your Savior or you are unsure of your salvation, today is the best time to confirm that important step in accepting God's favor for eternity.

**He is ahead of you . . . as your shepherd**
**He is behind you . . . as your rearguard.**
**He is above you . . . as your covering.**
**He is beneath you . . . as your foundation.**
**He is beside you . . . as your friend.**
**He is within you . . . as your life.**

Author unknown

*"For the Lord God is our Sun and our Shield. He gives us grace (favor) and glory. The Lord will withhold no good thing from those who do what is right."* Psalm 84:11 NIV

Blessings!

## 40

# WHAT IS YOUR MESSAGE?

April was puzzled recently by the odd messages she kept getting on her voice mail. Day after day, all she'd hear, from friends, family, and customers alike, would be their message and then they'd ALL say, "BEEP."

We were talking about something else and I had her check her voice mail message to find something out. She discovered the solution to the BEEP riddle.

Her message said, "I'm not available right now, so, please leave a beep after the message."

Isn't it interesting how we can be so easily misunderstood? We think our message is clear, but somehow there is a clinch in communication. In the humorous story above, we all get a little chuckle from it and then it's forgotten. But what about our life message? Are we presenting a clear message of who we are and what we believe to the world around us?

Do others know what you stand for? Do you? Is the message you want to convey to others clear? What words would people use to describe you? Write three words in the following blanks that you wish people would use to describe you: _____, _____, _____.

I think one of the worst things that can be said about a true Christ follower is—"I didn't know she was a Christian!" I don't believe we should be one of those pushy Christians who bombard everyone with their beliefs and are determined to "save" everyone they meet. People tend to walk the other way when they see them coming, even believers! However, we must make our life message clear because we are God's representatives here on planet Earth and He is counting on us to get His message to those whose hearts He is working in.

Look at 2 Corinthians 5:20.

As Christ followers, it is our great privilege to represent Father God in this way. We must be careful though to bring His message, not ours. In order for us to do that with the greatest effectiveness, we need to prepare ourselves through the studying of His Word and through the guidance of the Holy Spirit.

Our life message is sometimes called our personal testimony. What we say and how we act is very important because the world watches. What would likely happen if we didn't act the same Monday through Saturday as we do on Sunday? People would notice and think of us as a phony or a hypocrite and certainly not take our message seriously. I've known people who have stayed away from the church for years because they considered someone they knew from church to be a hypocrite.

Look at 1 Peter 3:15.
Has anyone ever asked you why you believe what you do or why you became a Christian?
If someone did ask you, what would you tell them in a sentence or two?
Do you think people can tell by your lifestyle that you are a Christian?
Do people act condemned in your presence? (Stop cussing or telling dirty jokes because you are there, etc.)
If you were forbidden to wear or show any Christian symbols or signs of your faith, how could you share your faith without using any words?

Look at John 13:34-35.
How important is it to show love in your Christian lifestyle?
One of the best ways to show your love for others is to treat them with kindness and respect, the way you would want to be treated. People respond

to acts of kindness. If you always have a ready smile, you will be perceived as approachable. And if others can see Jesus in you, they are more likely to hear what you have to say about what He has done in your life.

1 Corinthians 13 is called the "love chapter" and portions of it are read during some wedding ceremonies. Verses 4-8a. give a pretty complete description of God's definition of love. Look at this scripture and fill in the blanks with six of them. _____, _____, _____, _____, _____, _____.

Which of these virtues are easy for you to apply to your own lifestyle? _____ Which are the hardest? _____

When you approach people with love and with these virtues in place, they might not know what to do or how to receive the love and kindness you are offering. They will probably be very suspicious of you and they may even think you're nuts! They might be looking for an argument and are ready to do battle with you and in return you give them love—how crazy is that, they're thinking! It's not the normal way to react according to the world's view.

It might take us a little while to make it a habit to give love instead of giving someone a piece of your mind. It might take even longer to step back graciously when someone crowds in front of you. Put daily aggravations into proper perspective and choose to let the peace of God rule in your heart. These daily irritations can be made into opportunities to give honor to our Lord and Savior, Jesus Christ. Can you begin to imagine how shook up the devil would be if we begin to treat everyone with love and patience and acceptance?

The greatest enabler we can have in becoming true loving ambassadors of God on planet Earth is the Holy Spirit living in us. We don't have that ability in our natural selves. One of the fruit of the Spirit we have as Christ followers is love. We are responsible for nurturing and growing that fruit so that others can identify Jesus in us. This identification with Jesus is the foundation to making our message clear. Our earthly goal should be to be a difference-maker by pointing the way to Him.

For quite a while now, my habit before I get out of bed in the morning is to thank God for the good rest and the new day and sometimes I sing Him a little praise song and tell Him some things I have on my mind. Recently I've also begun to tell Him that I belong to Him. Of course He already knows that, but it's also a reminder for me. Knowing that I belong to God gives me confidence.

Psalm 57:7—*"My heart is fixed, O God, my heart is steadfast and confident! I will sing and make melody."* AMP

Another scripture says: *"In the reverent and worshipful fear of the Lord there is strong confidence, and His children shall always have a place of refuge."* Proverbs 14:26 AMP

Living out your faith can sometimes be scary. Especially, when your family or friends are not interested, think it's all right for you but not for them or are even hostile when God or Jesus is mentioned. But knowing who you are in God and what the Bible says about you will give you confidence.

The Bible says:

You are the *"light of the world."* (Matthew 5:14) We are to live in the world, opening up darkness to light to reveal what is right and what is best. Not in an aggressive or condemning way, but with quiet strength and love. Sometimes you are the only light in your workplace. Don't be discouraged and give up! You may be in that place, at this time for an eternal reason. Look around you and see what and who God sees.

You are the *"salt of the earth."* (Matthew 5:13) Our goal is to spice things up! Salt is also a preservative. Christ doesn't want anyone to perish, but all to come to a saving knowledge of Him and that should be our desire as well.

You are *"yeast and leaven."* (Matthew 13:33) God didn't leave us here on planet Earth to do nothing. He desire is for us to grow and mature in Him and help others to do the same.

You are *"the aroma of Christ."* (2 Corinthians 2:15) We are to be as a sweet perfume of love, service and truth among those who are perishing—to those who don't believe. (yet!) Some days it's hard to be sweet, I know, but the effort will be worth it when we get to heaven and see some of the people influenced by our sweet aroma!

Here are some questions to ponder:

Do you believe that God exists in three persons, Father, Son, and Holy Spirit?

Do you believe that Jesus Christ was born of a virgin? That He suffered, died, rose again and not sits at the right hand of the Father and will come back to planet Earth again?

Do you believe that the Holy Spirit dwells in you and every believer and is working in you and through you?

Do you believe Christians are to meet together regularly, united in the faith and live a righteous life in order to witness to the world about Jesus Christ?

Do you believe every word of the Bible?

Do you believe God will judge the world one day and take those whose hearts belong to Him with Him to heaven?

These are the basic beliefs of the Christian faith. You may be believing and living these beliefs without thinking much about them, but they may be the questions someone will ask you about one day. Be prepared to give an answer for the hope that you have in Jesus Christ.

Some time ago, God graciously gave me the following and I want to share it with you today:

Six words that the Lord is glad to hear are: 'Here I am Lord, use me."

If we say these words to Him with a truly sincere heart, He will at the end of our time on planet Earth, say these six words to us:

"Well done, good and faithful servant."

And that will make our hearts glad.

Blessings!

# 41

# THE PURSUIT OF HAPPINESS

For most of us, our aim in life is to be happy. Some of us would be happy if we could eat anything we want and not gain weight, others might want a new car or a bigger house and still others might feel the need to have a relationship restored, then we would be happy. Happiness comes in different forms.

There's an old saying that goes, "money can't buy happiness". We all know what it means—that true happiness comes from things that can't be found in any store, like love, friendship, and gratitude. But an article I read recently suggested that actually money can buy happiness—if you know where to spend it. And the article went on to say that joy can be affordable on any budget. Good news, right?

The rule is that you spend your dollars on things that further your goals and beliefs. A study revealed that if your money goes toward supporting things that you value such as honing a skill or hobby or redoing your garden or investing in some other interest, it is more satisfying because that helps to boost your feelings of self-worth.

I think this is pretty sound advice, but a new pair of shoes or a new lipstick is certainly a quick pick-me-up and also boosts the economy! Pick-me-ups are important, especially to sisters. Men might not understand this sisterhood principle, but that's OK. What was the last little pick-me-up you treated yourself to?

Material things, on the other hand, quickly lose their luster. Real satisfaction involves doing not buying. Doing usually involves people and the opportunity for things of eternal value.

People before things;
People before projects;
Family before friends;
Husband before children;
Husband before parents;
Tithe before wants;
Bible before opinions;
Jesus before all.

Another study I read found that the strongest sources of happiness are the people in our lives. People who are blessed to see their family often might take this blessing for granted. It wasn't too long ago that our Mary lived in the Florida Keys and our son, Dave and granddaughter, Mandy lived in Colorado. I actually questioned God on this unfair (I felt) situation. Someone told me that having your children scattered all over was a good way to see the country, so pretty often we took a trip either south or west! God supplied the finances for the trips, so I guess His answer was "just be patient I'm working on it."

That's not the same as a daily dose of family though, but our Jehovah-Jireh, (the Lord will provide) provided us with other people to fill in the gap. Friends, children of friends, nieces, and nephews, etc. God is so good to know exactly what we need. Now our daughter and our son are not only living back here in Michigan, but in our town.

Can you share a memorable, happy time you and your family had?

Blessings are defined as happy, fortunate, spiritually rich, a sense of well-being created by God's favor being shown on you, experiencing His grace, the feeling of joy regardless of outward circumstances, and so forth. If we consider that happiness can also be called blessings, then one of the times that made me happy and blessed was our Hephzibah Children's Home mission trips, in Macon, GA.

Doing for others has many rewards. One of the rewards is the friends we made as we were serving at the Children's Home. Another reward was the great friendships we made with the people on our missions team. Still another reward was the fulfillment of doing what I knew God called me to do. It's pretty scary to step out of your comfort zone, but whenever God calls you to do something He always provides the help you need to do it. Philippians 4:13 says that *"I can do all things through Christ who strengthens me"* (NKJV) He certainly did supply me with strength and everything else I needed for those trips.

What did God call you to do that was very rewarding and made you happy?
Let's look at some scriptures on happiness:
Isaiah 1:19
What are we to do that will result in happiness in our lives? Be _____ and _____. What does "eat from the best or the good of the land" mean to you?

Psalm 119:1-4
What makes us happy (or blessed) in these verses?
How does obedience make us happy?

1 Peter 5:6-7
Do you find it hard or easy to *"cast your cares on Him"*? Would it make you happy if you never had another problem to worry about here on planet Earth? Read the following story and see if you find similarities to your own life.

**"Most Christians are like a man who was toiling along the road, bending under a heavy burden, when a wagon overtook him, and the driver kindly offered to help him on his journey. He joyfully accepted the offer, but when seated in the wagon, continued to bend beneath his burden, which he still kept on his shoulders. "Why do you not lay down your burden?" asked the kind-hearted driver. "Oh!" replied the man, "I feel that it is almost too much to ask you to carry me, and I could not think of letting you carry my burden too."**

**And so Christians, who have given themselves into the care and keeping of the Lord Jesus, still continue to bend beneath the weight of their burdens, and often go weary and heavy-laden throughout the whole length of their journey." (source unknown)**

On a scale of one to ten (ten being the greatest) how much can you relate to this man?

Here is a little, but powerful prayer to use if you are serious about trusting the Lord with your concerns:

"Here, Lord, I give myself to You. I have tried to do things my way and messed everything up. I know what I ought to be and how I ought to manage my life, but I'm still miserable. My troubles, whether real or imagined, seem to get the best of me. Now I'm giving it all up to you and I mean it this time. Take possession of my life. Work in me all the good pleasure of Your will. Mold me and fashion me into a vessel for Your honor and use; and prepare me for every good work. Amen."

Read Matthew 11:28-30.

Does the idea of resting in the Lord appeal to you? Picture yourself exhausted after a long, hot day of painting your house or some other equally unappealing job. You approach your darkened bedroom and spy your very inviting looking bed. It was hours ago that you experienced the feel of this perfect, pleasantly refreshing, personal sanctuary. How delightful is the sensation of stretching out and relaxing every sore muscle and letting your body go in a perfect abandonment of ease and comfort! The strain of the day gone, for a few hours at least, and the busyness of the day has ceased. You no longer have to hold up an aching head or a weary back. You trust yourself to the bed with absolute confidence and it holds you up without effort or strain or even thought, on your part. You rest! You are happy and content!

Can that be a picture of resting in the Lord? Just as you've trusted your bed to give you rest, you turn your weary body over to the Lord to give you the rest you need. Only with God there is so much more. He will give you the physical refreshing that you need and He will also restore your spiritual being as well. (And it will last more than a few hours!) Let yourself go in a perfect abandonment of ease and comfort, trusting Him to hold you up and keep you safe. Your part is to simply rest. His part is to sustain you and He will not fail. That is the picture of resting in the Lord! That is true happiness!

Have you never experienced this perfect abandonment and contentment of resting in the Lord?

Happiness seems to be connected to a full and satisfying life. A life of purpose and doing things that makes others happy and content also. Jesus said He came that we might have life and have it to the full.

We've only touched the surface on the subject of happiness. The secret however is clear. Solomon wrote it in about 931 BC. He was the wisest man in the world, so we should read his words recorded in Ecclesiastes 12:13.

*"All has been heard; the end of the matter is: Fear God (revere and worship him, knowing that He is) and keep His commandments, for this is the whole of man (the full; original purpose of His creation, the object of God's providence, the root of character, the foundation of all happiness, the adjustment to all inharmonious circumstances and conditions under the sun) and the whole duty for every man."* AMP

Blessings!

# 42

# SMELLIN' LIKE A ROSE

Flowers are one of my favorite things. I find something I like in all kinds. Some have beautiful color like sunflowers or geraniums. Some are associated with the seasons like lilies and poinsettias. Others are known for their pretty little faces. (pansies) Some flowers even have personalities like impatiens and snapdragons! One thing flowers all have in common is that they all have some kind of fragrance. Some scents are pleasing such as roses and some not so pleasing like marigolds. But all flowers have value. Our God who likes variety made all of these different kinds of flowers to pretty up our world and whether I'm looking at a tulip or a daisy or a dandelion, I praise Him for it!

Our God who likes variety, made all of us different also. Some of us prefer bright colors and others dress in pastels. Some of us are worriers and some seem to take life head on. Some of us are naturally blond and some aren't. Some of us like to mingle and be with others and some are more likely to hang out at home. The list goes on and on, but all of us have a fragrance about us. I'm not talking about the perfume we did or didn't put on this morning. I'm talking about the fragrance of influence and all of us are wearing it!

The way our influence affects others can be like a marigold . . . harsh, not pleasant, even annoying or we can inspire, encourage, support and be a sweet aroma to those around us . . . smellin' like a rose.

Our fragrance or influence then is a testimony to all we come in contact with. Look at 2 Corinthians 2:14-17.

As we see in these verses, we who are Christ followers are the very fragrance of Christ and the seriousness of it means life and death to the ones we influence. We might say no way! I just have to be me and I don't want to be an influence on anyone. Since none of us live on a deserted island, sticking our heads in the sand is not an option.

As we look at these interesting facts about fragrance and how perfumes are made, think how it parallels our own Christian walk and its fragrance or influence.

It can take years to develop a new fragrance and the secret in a successful one is in the orchestration of select ingredients.

As many as 300 ingredients may be included to create a new perfume.

Fragrance notes are how perfumers describe single, unblended odors. A perfume is composed of three notes.

Top notes make the initial impact. They hit your nose first and burn off the fastest. Citruses are almost always top notes.

Middle notes determine the character of a perfume and tend to be floral. These fragrances are what your nose picks up after a few moments.

The bottom notes are the longest lasting scents and produce the foundation. Usually sandalwood, musk or vanilla are bottom notes because they have a lasting quality and influence the rate of evaporation.

A quality perfume has staying power. Its scent unfolds from the top note and each succeeding note reveals itself in harmony.

Many new fragrances are introduced each year, but only a few withstand the whims of fashion, reaching the timeless status of a classic.

Just as it can take years to develop a successful perfume that attracts buyers, so also it takes time for us to develop into successful Christ followers who attract non believers with our actions and words. What do you think a non believer is attracted to the most?

How can we be "real" and still be "godly"?

What is the cost of being real and godly at the same time?

What are the "select ingredients" of a person who has that godly quality of a *"sweet aroma in Christ"*?

The top note makes the initial impact. What first draws someone to a person who is a Christ follower?

The middle note determines the character of a perfume. What determines our character in our Christian walk?

The bottom notes are the longest lasting scents of the fragrance. What qualities are important to you in a person who professes to be a Christian?

I think we would all agree that being real is important if we are going to influence people in the right way. People who pretend to be something they are not won't fool others for very long. Here's a story to illustrate the point:

"There was a man who had been out of work for a long time and decided to inquire at the local zoo. He told the zookeeper, "I would like a job. I will clean cages. I will do whatever you need." The zookeeper said, "I'm sorry. We would love to hire you, but there just aren't any openings right now." Noticing how big and burly the man was, the zookeeper suddenly had an idea.

He said, "This is crazy, and you don't have to agree to it, but would you be willing to put on a costume and pretend to be a gorilla? Our gorilla died last week. He was our most popular exhibit. If you will be the gorilla, we will have a suit custom-made for you. We'll pay you really well."

Desperate for work, the man took the job. Feeling a little apprehensive on his first day, he put on the gorilla suit and climbed into the cage. He made a few gorilla moves and beat his chest a little. The people loved it.

The next day, he tried shaking the bars, screaming, and running around. The crowds started growing. By the third day, he was really enjoying his job and began swinging on the vines. But he swung too far, went over the wall, and landed in the middle of the lion's cage.

The lion turned and walked toward him rather quickly. The man knew that if he called for help, people would discover he wasn't really a gorilla. But if he kept quiet, he would be the lion's lunch. So he screamed, "Help!" "Shut up, stupid!" the lion whispered back. "You'll get us both fired!"

Pretenders don't last, whether it is in fiction or in real life. Our time is so short here on planet Earth that we don't have time to be something we are not. One of the things that keep us on track is studying the Word of God. It is there that we will find the wisdom and insights that we can use as guidelines for our lives as well as teaching truths to others along the way.

Make it your life's goal to always be teachable. There is always something we don't know or don't understand. Jesus sent the Holy Spirit to be our Teacher and our Guide. You will be greatly blessed if you ask for His guidance before you open your Bible. Here are some verses to prepare you to spread that sweet aroma that we talked about at the beginning of this study. Read and discuss for further insight:

John 14:26

Teaching and reminding are two of the functions of the Holy Spirit. What has been your experience when you've called on Him for this purpose?

1 Peter 3:15

Write out a sentence or two about how you feel about your faith journey and how it began.

2 Peter 3:18

What is the command here?

Colossians 1:9-10

This is a wonderful prayer that Paul prayed for the Colossians. What would it be like if everyone of our church family prayed that prayer for each other? What would it be like if our universal church family prayed that prayer for each other?

2 Corinthians 6:1

What does this scripture call us? _____ How does God's grace help us as we do the things we are called to do?

James 1:22-24

What is the danger of just listening to the Word and not doing what it says?

Psalm 86:11

Some words to describe undivided are: complete, full, whole and total. What are we missing if our hearts are divided?

Daniel 12:3

The phrase, "lead many to righteousness" refers to leading someone to Christ and if you have ever had that glorious experience, you'll not only shine like the stars, but you'll be walking on clouds as well!

Dear Lord,

You sent Your Son Jesus to die on a cross for me. He endured indignity, suffering and death so that I might live. Because He lives, I, too, have Your promise of eternal life. Let me today and every day that I remain on planet Earth look for opportunities to share the message of Jesus Christ through my words, attitudes, and actions. Allow me the boldness to spread the sweet aroma of the fragrance of Christ to my world of influence. Amen.

Blessings!

## 43

# YOUR MIND—DO YOUR THOUGHTS REALLY MATTER?

Every thought that we think is either negative or positive. It's a choice. Whenever you are weighed down with a negative thought, just say, "Cancel, cancel." Don't speak this thought out loud, because once you do, you under-line it, you underscore that negative thought. So just cancel it.

Negative thoughts will turn into negative attitudes and actions if you let them and that can affect everyone around you.

In most homes, the mother sets the mood for the entire family. When she appears satisfied and cheerful, her husband and children will likely emulate her attitude; unfortunately, her negative moods are also contagious. And you know as well as I do that . . . IF MAMA AIN'T HAPPY, AIN'T NOBODY HAPPY!

Look up Proverbs 23:7a and write in the space below:


We can see how important it is to cancel wrong or negative thinking and replace it with God approved thinking. In Romans 12:2 we learn that we are to be completely renewed in our minds and attitudes so we can prove for ourselves the good and perfect will of God. God has a plan and purpose for each one of us, but we won't experience those plans if we stick to our old way of thinking.

The more mature in the faith we become, the easier it is to look at things God's way. Let's look at the way our thinking and God's thinking differ.

At one time in our lives, we may have come upon a stumbling block or an impossible situation—in our estimation anyway. But if we look in our Bibles we'll find God's thoughts about the impossible. Look at Luke 18:27. The Bible has recorded so many impossible things made possible by God that He is called "The God of the Impossible." Name a few of the Biblically "impossible things He's made possible."

Some days we may feel unloved and want to throw a "pity party" for one. God loves us with an unfailing love. We all can quote John 3:16 as the greatest act of love. Here are some other verses that show His love for us: Isaiah 54:10, 1 John 4:16-19 and if you really need a big dose of His love that "endures forever," read Psalm 136!

When you have those few and far between "down" times and think no one really cares, read 1 Peter 5:7. This verse tells us to present all of our worries, anxieties, and problems to God. Does that sound like no one cares? God does. And others do too. It's just that negative thinking we all sometimes have that trips us up. Can you relate?

Often when we have these negative feelings, God gives us grace to overcome. It may be that the reason we have negative feelings is because we are going through some negative stuff. It happens here on planet Earth! However we aren't to expect abundant grace and favor and blessings in every situation because sometimes it doesn't fit into God's divine plan for us. We may be more valuable to Him in the difficult situation than if He removes us from it.

Read James 1:12. What is the promise there?

In 2 Corinthians 12, Paul prayed for the Lord to take "this thorn" from him. God chose not to and He gave His reason in verse 9. Look at it now.

We may think it's not possible to continue, but the grace God gives us in the trial is sufficient. Be thankful that He doesn't give us everything we think we need when we think we need it. How can we grow if all things were simple and trouble-free? Think of the life-growing lessons we would miss!

When you come to a crossroads in your life, what is your first step? Do you spent hours and hours trying to figure things out? Do you ask other people's opinion? Or do you ask Father God for wisdom? James 1:5 says that—*"If any of you lacks wisdom, let him ask of God, who gives to all liberally and without reproach, and it will be given to him."* NKJV

Our Father God has a life plan for each of us. He is willing and able to direct our steps. Here are a few verses on the subject: Proverbs 20:24, Psalm 37:23, and Jeremiah 29:11. Don't ever think that God is not interested in the decisions you make in life. That's negative and false thinking.

Some of us have guilty thoughts from past circumstances and we can't seem to forgive ourselves from the wrong things we've done. We are so down on ourselves that we think God won't forgive our past sins either. Yes, He will. Forgiveness is as simple as asking with a sincere and contrite heart. Look at 1 John 1:9 and Psalm 103:12.

As you can see the Bible is rich in ways that we can change our thoughts and attitudes. Begin to think positively in your life. The more you study the Word and know the principles that God has set for us, the quicker positive thoughts will come. Even if whatever is going on in your life right now is not good, expect God to bring good out of it, because that is what He promised to do. (Romans 8:28 and other places)

Worry is a negative thought practice that we are all familiar with. The modern term for that practice is **stinking thinking!** When you find yourself doing it, immediately say—**cancel, cancel!**

Worry distracts us from doing our work for the day, caring for our family, may even affect our health and it also paralyzes the good things that God wants to work out in our lives. Worry equals no trust. There are many scriptures that encourage us not to worry, but to trust in the Lord.

Here are a few to look up and discuss:

Matthew 6:31-34
Psalm 73:28
Proverbs 3:5-6
Psalm 46:1
Psalm 118:8-9
Psalm 121:1-2

**Trust the past to God's mercy, the present to God's love, and the future to God's providence. St. Augustine**

Here's something to think about: As we are working on getting rid of those pesky negative thoughts, we're bound to have some empty places to fill. (No I don't mean to call us empty headed!)

Satan will try to fill those empty places with negative thoughts when we least expect it. Just when we think we're being a positive, uplifting, encouraging, sweet spiritual person . . . . bam! Some little disturbing thing happens and we lose our cool.

An excellent verse to memorize for occasions like this is Philippians 4:8. Write it in the space below and begin to memorize it if you haven't all ready.

It's not so much what happens to us as how we react to what happens that makes the difference. Cultivate the happy side of life. Find humor in situations. Often when we look back, we see that things happened for the best or that God truly made something good come from a not so good situation.

Live in an attitude of gratitude. Count your blessings. Even better tell people what God has done for you. It will make you feel great and God receives the honor.

Blessings!

# 44

# WOMEN FROM THE BIBLE—WOMEN JUST LIKE US?

Every day we are faced with new circumstances and challenges. But the Bible says that there is nothing new under the sun. We can learn from the women of the Bible because the more we hear about their individual life stories, the more we realize they are women just like us. Customs and cultures are different than ours, of course, but basically the lives of God's people held the same challenges then as now.

Three women that I want us to learn from today are:
Martha, because of her gift of service.
Hannah, who was a women of prayer and perseverance.
Abigail, a very wise and discerning woman.

Read Luke 10:38-42
What do you think was Martha's main spiritual gift?
What do you think was Mary's main spiritual gift?

Many people read this story of the two sisters and their different attitudes and generally think it's better to be a Mary than a Martha. (So do I.) But truthfully, we need Marthas in this world too.

Martha was the oldest of the three siblings and probably a widow and the owner of the house they lived in. This family was special to Jesus. They were His friends and was often a guest in their home. It was expensive to entertain Jesus, because he didn't come alone. He always brought twelve other guys with Him. But Martha was generous by nature and didn't consider the expense, but felt it an honor.

With all the responsibilities of being the hostess on her shoulders, how could have Martha handled things differently?

In verse 42 what is the "one thing" that Jesus is talking about?

I believe that the lesson to be learned from Martha is that we need a balance in our lives. It is a good thing to honor your guests by making everything nice, pleasant and lovely in all the little details. But not at the cost of things with eternal value, those are the things that last. We must determine how God wants us to serve Him and put a great value on those things.

Look up John 9:4 and write below.

Time is short. We should feel the urgency and do the work that God has assigned to us.

I think Martha did learn this lesson. Look at John 11:25-27.

With this great confession of faith, Martha showed that she had balanced the works of her hands with the faith of her heart. We also need to find that balance in our spiritual walk. Focus on things of eternal value.

Hannah's story is told in the first 2 chapters of a book bearing her son's name—1 Samuel. Being childless was considered a major tragedy in ancient Israel. This was the most dreaded fear of every woman in a culture where sons determined a woman's worth. To be without a male child virtually guaranteed women a pauper's widowhood. To be without any child was guaranteed curse of God.

Other women of Old Testament times were barren, but God in His great mercy, gave them a child. Some examples are Sarah (mother of Isaac) Rebekah (mother of Esau and Jacob) and Rachel (mother of Joseph and Benjamin.)

Read 1 Samuel 1:1-7

As if being childless wasn't enough, what made Hannah's situation worse? What do you think Peninnah's motives were for taunting Hannah?

Read verses 9-11

When we are hurt by the words of others, our greatest temptation is to talk about our feelings or to "get back" at that person. What does Hannah do? Why is this so significant?

Read verses 12-18

How can you explain verse 18, considering that nothing tangible has changed and Hannah will be returning to the same home with the same people and problems?

Hannah's comfort and encouragement in this difficult situation came from *"pouring out her soul to the Lord."* (verse15) It was by spending time in God's presence that she regained the strength to face Peninnah.

When we are in difficult circumstances, God's presence is where we can find comfort and strength to face the challenge and come out on the other side victorious!

We cannot control the amount of time we have on planet Earth, but we can control what we will be remembered for.

We cannot control the shape and features of our face, but we can control our expressions.

We cannot control someone else's opportunities, but we can seek our own.

We cannot control another person's annoying faults, but we can see that we do not develop irritating practices.

We cannot control someone else's relationship to God, but we can be sure about our own salvation.

Of all of the Old Testament women, Abigail was considered to be the wisest. She was also known to be a peacemaker and a woman of good understanding. She had a great influence for good and helped David in his fugitive days as he was running and hiding from Saul to remember that he was God's anointed as the future king of Israel.

Read 1 Samuel 25:2-13

How does verse 3 describe Abigail?

How does verse 3 describe Nabal?

Nabal was one of the richest men in the area and it was sheep-shearing season at their home when some of David's men came for food. Many guests had gathered and there was much feasting. Abigail had provided abundantly for her guests for she was a woman who had a reputation for gracious hospitality.

David's request for food was not uncommon. He and his men provided protection to Nabal's men and property and so it was natural to expect some provisions in return.

When one of the servants reported to Abigail what Nabal said to David's men and confirmed to her that David and his men did indeed protect Nabal's men and flocks when they were out in the fields, she quickly organized food and provisions to help make things right.

Read verses 19-25
Who did Abigail send to David with the food?
What was Abigail's attitude in these difficult circumstances?

Read verses 26-35
We see as this part of Abigail's story ends that she has words of wisdom and encouragement for David. This is an example of grace under fire. No matter what our circumstances at home or at work, we need to not let the situations hinder us, but to work out the situations with the heart of an over comer through the guidance of the Holy Spirit. Do not step down to the level of your circumstances, but lift them to your own high calling in Christ.

*"But the wisdom that comes from heaven is first of all pure; then peaceloving, considerate, submissive, full of mercy and good fruit, impartial and sincere."* James 3:17 NIV

List the 8 things that godly wisdom is:

1
2
3
4

5
6
7
8

Martha, Hannah, and Abigail, none were perfect, but all were striving to become woman who would influence their world in a positive, godly way... women just like us.

Blessings!

# 45

# PROMISES—HIS WORD IS TRUE

PROMISE (prom is) a declaration made by one person to another to do, or to refrain from doing, a thing; a declaration which gives the person receiving it the right to expect the performance of the thing or its non-performance according to the nature of the declaration.

God's promises are different than man's promises to us in 2 ways:
1. God is altogether trustworthy. (Psalm 18:30) Man may sometimes forget or for some other reason not keep his promise.
2. God's promises are always in accordance to our own good. Man's promises may not always have our best interest in mind.

The children's chorus that says:

"Every promise in the book is mine, every chapter, every verse, every line" . . .

But the fact is many of God's promises go unclaimed because we have to know the promise before we can claim it as ours. We either don't know our Bibles well enough or else we read it and think the promise is not for us personally.

It's true that many of the promises are written for a particular person, nation or situation in mind, but if our Heavenly Father who loves each of us unconditionally has done something for a Bible character, how can we think He won't do the same for us if we ask? According to Ephesians 6:9, God has no favorites.

But we mustn't force any and every Bible promise into our specific situation. Is the promise meant for a unique situation and given to a specific person or group who lived in the days in which Scripture was being written? Or is the promise one of the many general promises that has a much broader meaning? We need to check the context of the passage and use discernment.

An example of a promise to a specific individual in a unique situation would be God's promise to Joshua in Joshua 6, when he and his men were to march around Jericho. Think of the consequences if that promise was fulfilled in any person who requested it!

Another example is the promise in Mark 16:18. Look at it and discuss with the group. This is probably not a promise for anyone other than the time and situation as well. We are responsible to know our Bible and not take any one verse out of context.

However if the promise is a universal one, then count on it, believe it, memorize it. It could prove to be a great source of comfort and reassurance in the days ahead. Here are some examples to look up and read:

Psalm 103:11-13 ... What wonderful words from our loving heavenly Father. How do these verses make you feel as a child of God?

Proverbs 3:5-6 ... In order to fully accept that God is true to His word, we must fully trust Him.

Isaiah 41:10 ... This is a great promise for courage and strength, a good verse to memorize. Can you think of times when this verse whispered in prayer can make a difference in a situation?

Matthew 7:7-8 ... Our Father knows our needs and desires, but He wants us to ask. He wants us to be dependent on Him.

Even with those promises we may claim however, we need further discernment to determine whether they are conditional or unconditional.

A conditional promise has 2 parts, ours and God's and won't be fulfilled until we have done our part.

# AM I MY SISTER'S KEEPER?

Look up Psalm 37:4 and write below.

What is our part?

What is God's part?

God is talking about a heart that is committed to Him—not American Express. We have to read more of this passage to get the meaning of verse 4—read verses 1-6.

What does "delight yourself in the Lord" mean?

If we are God-centered then what would the desires of our heart most likely be?

(See Micah 6:8 to find the attributes of a godly man/woman)

When our hearts are in tune with God, I believe He will give us our desires, because they will be in accordance with His plan for us. And we must trust Him to know what's best for us since He knows the future and we don't.

If it's not, we can trust Him to NOT let us have the thing. We can be secure in the knowledge God wants what is best for us.

Ever pray for something and end up very thankful that you DIDN'T get it? Share if you are able.

Look at Isaiah 65:24

Ever hear the quote: **"God always answers prayer. Sometimes the answer is yes, sometimes no, and sometimes the answer is wait."** This promise in Isaiah assures us that, yes, God will hear and answer our prayer.

I've prayed for a certain thing to happen for years, but haven't seen the answer yet. Sometimes the timing is not right for the answer to come. Or if there are other people involved, God is waiting on them. He doesn't force His will on people, even if it's for their own good. One thing I have learned though and that is I should never give up and stop praying.

## PUSH ~~ Pray Until Something Happens!

What is the one thing these verses promise to the believer who asks?

Deuteronomy 33:25

Philippians 4:13

Isaiah 40:31

Nehemiah 8:10

Besides strength, what are some of the other benefits of these promises to us as believers?

Look up and write below: 2 Peter 3:9

This is a promise I often use when I'm praying for someone's salvation. I'm simply reminding God of what He has said in His Word.
We can intercede more effectively if we use God's words and promises to us.

One of God's attributes is patience as we read in 2 Peter 3:9. Look at Nehemiah 9:17b for some of His other attributes and list below.

Does knowing some of these attributes make it easier to claim God's promises? Why?

Has God given you a verse that you feel is a special promise He wrote just for you? One that you have claimed for a certain situation? Share if you are able.

In 2 Corinthians 1:20 we read: *"For no matter how many promises God has made, they are "yes" in Christ. And so through Him the "amen" is spoken by us to the glory of God."* (NIV)

As believers and Christ followers, we have already received many of God's promises through our Lord and Savior, Jesus Christ. One of the promises is eternal life (1 Timothy 4:8). Another promise is of the Holy Spirit (Acts 1:4 and Ephesians 1:13). We also have received the amazing promise of rest for our souls (Hebrews 4:1) and the promise of truth and spiritual freedom (John 8:32-36)

One of my favorite promises is found in Hebrews 13:5 which says " ... *never will I leave you, never will I forsake you."*(NIV)

As you are reading and studying your Bible and you come across a promise that speaks to your heart, underline it in your Bible. Even better, make a list in the front or back of your Bible of special promises. This will enable you to refresh your memory on those days when you need a quick word of encouragement. As you know, sisters, we all have those days!

Blessings!

# 46

# TO REJOICE IS A CHOICE

Definition of optimism: "A cheerful frame of mind that enables a tea kettle to sing though in hot water up to its nose."

I admire a person who can have a positive attitude even though her life may not be in the happiest of circumstances at the moment. Such a person, if she is a Christian, is allowing God time to do His work in those circumstances. This is a person who is not willing to let her feelings rule her life, but to trust the circumstance to God. It's a choice we all have to make when things don't go the way we want them to.

It is human nature for unpleasant situations to get us down and I'm not saying that we should put on a phony smile at all times. That's completely unrealistic and people would probably think there's something wrong with us. Here's what I am saying: positive thinking knocks negative thinking out of the box every time. We will reap good results if we only hang in there and rejoice in the Lord as we go through those valleys we all experience while living on planet earth.

The story of Paul and Silas singing in prison is a really good example of rejoicing in not so good circumstances. Let's read the account in Acts 16:22-26.

Notice that Paul and Silas were beaten and flogged, but that wasn't enough punishment for the crime of healing a demon possessed girl. Next they were thrown into jail with their backs sore and raw, and not just jail, but the inner most part of the jail. One commentary said that the inner jail was most likely the dungeon. Then to insure that they didn't get away, their feet were put in stocks. To say that they were uncomfortable in their present situation would be an understatement!

All this for what we would consider a good deed. Who of us wouldn't shout to the roof tops at the unfairness of it all? But not Paul and Silas, because while they were in that dark, smelly prison with mean, violent and unfriendly prisoners they: (circle correct letter)

- A. They cried
- B. They recited the 23rd Psalm
- C. They sang praises to God

Verse 25 says that about midnight, they were praying and singing loud enough for all the other prisoners to hear them. How could they find the strength and energy to do that?

It states in the Word that God inhabits the praises of His people (Psalm 22:3) so I believe that God was with them there in the dungeon. There's certainly a lesson in that for us. I believe that praise is a spiritual weapon to be used to ward off the enemy. Paul and Silas were experiencing persecution for their religious beliefs. In using praise as a weapon, and because of their faith, God was able to defeat the enemy and turn the situation completely around.

Unscramble the words and fill in the blanks that tell us what happened next while Paul and Silas were imprisoned. (Acts 16:26)

"And (EUYLNDSD)_____ there was a(AETRG)_____

(EAUAEKQHTR)_____, so that the (OIAUOSNT DNF)_____

of the prison were(EANKHS)_____: and immediately all the doors were (EEODNP)

_____, and everyone's chains came (EOOSL)_____."

Paul and Silas had a choice to rejoice or have a pity party. They chose the way that ultimately benefited them and glorified the Lord. Reacting the way they did also enabled them to influence and impress their jailer so much that he wanted what he could see they had. The end result was that the jailer and his whole family were won to the Lord. Can you imagine how their lives were changed?

I wonder, don't you, if some of those prisoner's lives were influenced for God. They probably had been laughing and ridiculing those men of God, but after the earthquake, they weren't laughing anymore! It's likely that some of those prisoners were converted, but only the conversion of the jailer was recorded. I guess we'll have to wait 'til we get to Heaven for the rest of the story.

Does this attitude of rejoicing whatever the circumstances seem unrealistic to you? I'm not made that way, you say. Well, if you think that, then consider this—the Spirit of God has put in you the fruit of the Spirit, which includes the seed of joy. Whether or not we use this joy ability is our choice. God must want us to use it since He put this capability of joy within each one of us. Since He has been gracious enough to give us this ability, I think we are causing Him to grieve if we don't at least attempt to use this joy gift.

Let's find encouragement from this verse in Isaiah 30:18 AMP . . .

*"And therefore the Lord (earnestly) waits (expecting, looking, and longing) to be gracious to you; and therefore He lifts Himself up, that He may have mercy on you and show loving-kindness to you. For the Lord is a God of justice. Blessed (happy, fortunate, to be envied) are all those who (earnestly) wait for Him, who expect and look and long for Him (for His victory, His favor, His love, His peace, His joy, and His matchless, unbroken companionship)!"*

God is not just looking for someone to bless, but He is longing to extend grace and mercy to you and me. But guess what? He can't do His work in a negative atmosphere. He wants to bless someone who is looking expectantly for Him to do His mighty work. Let's be sure that someone is us!

Let us teach ourselves to choose to rejoice by filling our thoughts with scripture verses that talk about the benefits God desires to give us. If we would begin the day by reading this verse we just read, would that make a difference in our outlook on life? Go back and read this verse to yourself and circle the benefits you see. What are they?

To some of us, having an attitude of gratitude might not be easy because of our background. To others, it may come natural. Either way, God will honor our efforts to see Him in all things and to look for the good in difficult circumstances. This attitude is surely one that will glorify and bless Him.

Look at these verses and discuss the benefits to us in each one.

Proverbs 15:13
Proverbs 15:15
John 14:3
John 14:27
Proverbs 17:22
John 10:10b
Proverbs 16:3
2 Corinthians 12:9
1 John 5:13

The best way to honor God is to live a life of thanksgiving. As you can see from these verses, we will benefit greatly as we are living the life God desires for us. Today, may we find time to lift our thankful hearts to Him. He is worthy of our praise.

Blessings!

# 47

# GIVE THANKS WITH A GRATEFUL HEART

A famous author, good storyteller and great Christian lady was Erma Bombeck. Here's what she wrote about Thanksgiving:

"There's a parallel between the holiday of Thanksgiving and families. Families are not the Fourth of July, with brilliant flashes that light up the sky (though they make a few fireworks from time to time.) Families are not Halloween—there are no masks to hide behind. Families aren't Easter, Christmas, or New Year's either. But families are Thanksgiving

Thanksgiving is honest and simple, warm and natural. It's setting the table at Mom's house and feeling like a child again. It's having Dad try to simultaneously be sociable and watch football on TV. It's hearing Mom say, "You cook for two days and it's over in 20 minutes." It's hearing everyone say, "I ate too much!" It's all very predictable—and very wonderful. Thanksgiving is a time for families to come together, to reflect, and to be thankful that they are..."

I don't know if you agree with Erma or not. Some things are the same in most families at Thanksgiving, especially the part about cooking for 2 days and it's over in 20 minutes! Now and then I think it's all about the turkey and not enough about the thankful part. I think sometimes that the thankful part comes when we've cleaned up the mess, the leftovers are in the refrigerator and we are tucked in our beds, ready to drift off to dreamland, thankful that another Thanksgiving Day is over!

By the way, did you know that the first Thanksgiving Day was celebrated in 1621, near Plymouth, Massachusetts, following their first harvest? But this feast most people refer to as the first Thanksgiving was never repeated. Oddly enough, most devoutly religious pilgrims observed a day of thanksgiving with prayer and fasting, not feasting. Yet even though this harvest feast was never called Thanksgiving by the pilgrims of 1621, it has become the model for the traditional Thanksgiving celebrations in America. (world-wide web)

You don't need me to tell you that giving thanks to God should not be a once a year event. We all fall short when it comes to giving thanks to the Lord with a grateful heart. When we were children, our mothers taught us to be polite and say thank you. Why do we take God's goodness to us for granted? We know that as believing, growing, serving Christ followers, we are blessed beyond measure. Thanksgiving should become a daily habit, a regular part of our daily routine. The time to be thankful is now!

Let's face it, there is no way we can offer the kind of gratitude that would truly be worthy of what the Lord has done for us. The only words that would even come close to showing our thankfulness to Him are His own words. Let's look at some of them:

Hebrews 12:28 from the NASB tells us, *"Therefore, since we receive a kingdom which cannot be shaken, let us show gratitude by which we may offer to God an acceptable service with reverence and awe . . ."*

One of the great ways to show gratitude is to pass it on. We are so blessed that we would be remiss if we didn't bless someone in the ways the Lord has bestowed blessings on us. Our lives are rich in the blessings we receive from God. How much richer would we be when we share them with others?

Look at 1 Thessalonians 5:18 and fill in the blanks. This is the manner in which Father God wants us to be thankful.

"In _____ give thanks; for this is God's _____ for _____ in Christ Jesus." NKJV

Does it come natural for you to say thank-you or do you need to work on it?

This verse is a good verse to begin your day: *"This is the day the Lord has made; we will rejoice and be glad in it."* Psalm 118:24 NKJV

If you start your day with this verse, how will that benefit you?

The Bible is full of blessings and benefits. Often we are so busy with the stuff in our lives that we miss these blessings, but they are there for us all the same. I've listed a few of these blessings here. As you look at them praise the Lord for His goodness. Which ones mean the most to you?

T ... Transforming power ... Psalm 40:2

H ... His holiness ... Revelation 4:8b

A ... Alleluia! For my salvation ... Romans 10:9-10

N ... New life ... 2 Corinthians 5:17

K ... Keeping power ... John 10:28

S ... Shelter from my enemy ... Psalm 61:3

G ... Gift of His Son! ... 2 Corinthians 9:15

I ... Inner peace ... John 14:27

V ... Victory ... 1 Corinthians 15:57

I ... Inheritance ... Colossians 1:12

N ... Never ending love ... Psalm 107:1

G ... God's goodness ... 1 Chronicles 16:34

Just a few things we should be thankful for this day and every day!

As we plan, shop, clean, and cook for this year's Thanksgiving Day, let us continually remind ourselves to thank the Lord for the many blessings and opportunities He has provided for us during the past year. And as a blessing to Him, let's make our Thanksgiving Day more about Him than turkey and football.

*"Let us continually offer the sacrifice of praise to God, that is, the fruit of our lips, giving thanks to His Name."* Hebrews 13:15 NKJV

Blessings!

# 48

# GOOD THINGS

Martha Stewart in her magazine always included a list of things that were in her opinion, "good things". For instance, some good things might have been a freshly iron shirt, a perfectly arranged bouquet of flowers, or a complete and alphabetized list of the current books on your book shelf, which was organized by color. ☺

We all can make a list of the things we feel are "good things." Mine would include, a sunny, warm, (but not hot) summer day, looking at my flower garden after I weeded it, chocolate of any kind, a good book and a long afternoon or spending the day with my husband.

What are some of your "good things"?

There are a lot of good things in the Bible. Maybe that's why it's called the Good Book! Look at Psalm 84:11.

What is God described as in this verse?_____ and _____. Why is this a good thing?

What does the Lord bestow in this verse? _____ and _____.

Have you been on the receiving end of these things?

He does not withhold any good thing from those whose _____ is _____.

The word "good" is described as something that is excellent, profitable, or morally right; advancement of prosperity or well-being; something useful or beneficial. Would you agree that it would be to our best interests if God would grant "good things" to us?

I have found that as we are living our day to day lives, trying to follow His precepts and being obedient to the Holy Spirit's guidance that many good things will come into our lives.

What have been your experiences in receiving God's good things? Name a few.

God's good things are called blessings and if we take a moment to think about it, we would realize that we have more blessings than we can count. In fact, a good habit to get into is to remind yourself of the day's blessings before you go to sleep each night.

God always has a better plan. His timing is perfect; He is never too early and never too late. His principles are in place for our well-being. Knowing the scriptures and applying them to our lives, makes life easier and more peaceful. He will always make something good from the messed-up things in our lives. (It is up to us to look for the good in these things.) The Old Testament account of Joseph's life is a good example of this.

Because Joseph was the favorite son of Jacob, his brothers envied and were jealous of him. One day they secretly sold him as a slave to a band of merchants, who took him to Egypt. Then they told their father that Joseph was dead. In Egypt, Joseph was again sold to Potiphar, a high government official. God showed favor to him and he rose to power and influence in Potiphar's household until one day Potiphar's wife tried to seduce him. When he refused, he was thrown in jail on false charges.

In prison, Joseph again was shown God's favor and he had a great amount of influence there as well. One day the King wanted an interpretation of his dreams and Joseph was sent for. After Joseph interpreted his dreams, the King made him a ruler in the land, second only to himself. After a time there was famine in the land and in the regions around Egypt as well. Joseph was well prepared and Egypt had food with plenty to sell to the neighboring countries.

One day his brothers came to buy food for the family and after several audiences with them, Joseph made himself known to them. The brothers were afraid and rightly so. But Joseph didn't want revenge, he forgave his brothers and the whole family moved to Egypt.

Many unfair things happened in Joseph's life, but God's goodness and mercy was obvious. Joseph was faithful to God and God was faithful to him. Look at Joseph's words to his brothers in Genesis 50:19-20. What is the key thought in those verses?

When Joseph's life was being messed-up and people were falsely accusing him, he chose the high road and believed that God would take care of the situations. What do you think kept him from becoming bitter and resentful?

Explain why Romans 8:28 is a good verse to go along with Joseph's life story.

We may at some point in our lives be falsely accused of something. The best way to deal with an unfortunate situation as that is to stay the course and let God take care of it. It will probably be hard and your human side will want to get even. Be confident of this: God is watching and nothing slips past Him. If your heart attitude is right and you continue to persevere, He will bring many blessings into your life. Just continue to keep on keeping on and watch for God to work.

Look at these verses from the NIV and fill in the blanks.

Isaiah 41:13:
"For I am the Lord, your God who takes hold of your right hand and says to you, _____ ; I will _____ you."

Psalm 55:22:
"Cast your_____ on the Lord and He will sustain you; He will _____ let the righteous _____."

2 Chronicles 15:7:
But as for you, be _____ and do not _____, for your work will be rewarded."

What does John 10:10b have to say about why Jesus came?

What does Proverbs 30:5 state about God's word?
What other benefit does it tell us?

Not all of the things that happen to us in this life are good or beneficial. That's because this is called planet Earth, not Heaven. The good thing we can count on though is that God loves us and protects us. In times of trouble, He comforts us; in times of sorrow, He dries our tears. In times of difficulty, He is as near to us as our next breath. He has promised to never leave us or forsake us and He is a Promise Keeper.

Here are some other good things (blessings) for the believer:

The Bible says that you are a child of God, (John 1:12) and Jesus' friend. (John 15:15) You have been redeemed and forgiven of all your sins (Col. 1:14) and cannot be separated from God's love. (Romans 8:35-39) You can be confident that God will finish the good work He started in you. (Phil. 1:6) You have not been given a spirit of fear, but of power, love and self discipline. (2 Tim. 1:7) You can find mercy and grace to help in time of need, (Hebrews 4:16) and you have direct access to God through the Holy Spirit. (Eph. 2:18) You have been chosen to bear fruit, (John 15:16) and are a personal, Spirit-empowered witness of Jesus Christ. (Act 1:8) You are a temple of God (1 Cor. 3:16) and His co-worker. (2 Cor. 6:1) You are God's workmanship, created for good works, (Eph. 2:10) and you can do all things through Christ who strengthens you. (Phil. 4:13) Wow! Talk about good things!

If you ever experience a season of low self-esteem or a time of depression, just go over this list or better yet commit it to memory. As a woman of God, you have every reason to have confidence in the One you've put your trust in.

One final good thing I want us to talk about today is the One who enabled us to be reconciled with Father God and that is our Savior, Jesus Christ. We know from scripture that He is now seated at the right hand of God, but He will return one day for those whose hope is in Him.

There is a thread running through the Bible from the Old Testament to the New Testament and that thread is Jesus Christ. There are well over 300 references to His return. Does this excite you?

To most of us, looking forward to Christ's return gives us comfort. To a casual, uncommitted, indifferent non-believer the thought of Christ's return must be pretty scary. If that is you, ask a Christian you know to introduce you to Jesus. He is waiting and the angels are ready to rejoice! God has given us the truth in His Word concerning His Son's return to prompt holy living, so that we will be ready at any moment to meet Him face to face. Here's what we are to do while we are waiting:

1 Corinthians 15:58:
*"Therefore, my beloved brethren, be steadfast, immovable, always abounding in the work of the Lord, knowing that your labor is not in vain in the Lord."*(NKJV)

And while we are standing firm, letting nothing in this life move us in the wrong direction, doing the work God has called us to do, what is Jesus doing? He is preparing for us a place in Heaven with Him. (John 14:2-3) That is a very good thing!

Blessings!

# 49

# COMMONSENSE FROM PROVERBS

Proverbs is a book (along with so much of the Bible) that you can read again and again and get something new every time. You will find wisdom there along with lots of good old commonsense. A lot of the advise there has a dose of humor. Here's an example from Proverbs 11:22: *"As a ring of gold in a swine's snout, so is a lovely woman who lacks discretion."* Truth served up with a little humor.

Many people read a chapter a day each month for their daily Bible reading. Pretty easy because there are 31 chapters, one for each day in most months. I like the Proverbs because it gives practical advice for every day living. For example:

A friend of yours likes to talk. When you are with her, there's never more than a moment or two of silence and that's because she's taking a bite or a drink or a breath. Some of her comments about people you both know are hilarious, but you feel kind of guilty when you laugh at the comical way she sees things. She keeps you entertained with all the silliness, but you wonder if maybe you should stop seeing her so often. Should you:

a. Tell her you'll only see her if she stops gossiping and making fun of your mutual friends and insist that she pray for forgiveness for all the trouble she may have caused by her loose tongue.
b. Ask five of your close mutual friends to plan an intervention to help her with this problem of hers.
c. Don't laugh at her funny stories, this will discourage her. Change the subject as soon as possible. Pray for strength and wisdom before you two meet. Know that you might have to give her up as a friend.

A good piece of advice for this situation is found in Proverbs 10:19. Look it up and fill in the blanks.

"When _____ are many, _____ is ____ _____, but he who holds his _____ is _____." NIV

Here are some other verses on the topic of gossip and careless talk. As we look at them, what lessons are there for us?

Proverbs 11:13
Proverbs 12:22
Proverbs 17:20
Proverbs 21:23
Proverbs 16:28

Those who know me know that I'm not against having fun and laughing. Laughter is good for us in many ways. An afternoon of gossip and silly chit-chat may seem harmless, but the truth is it is a real hazard to your relationship with family and friends and certainly your relationship with God suffers. It's just not worth the trouble and here's the reason:

When we make a habit of laughing at other people instead of with them, we are choosing death over life. In Proverbs 18:21 we read *"that the power of life and death is in the tongue and we eat the fruit of it."* When we choose to listen to gossip and loose talk, we are choosing an ungodly or unwholesome thing. As Christ followers, we are not to associate with things that are not God honoring. We wouldn't choose a rotten apple or a bunch of rotten grapes to eat would we? That wouldn't be good for our bodies just as unwholesome talk is not good for our spirits. Rotten fruit is yucky, so is sin.

Proverbs is all about wisdom. The wisest man in the world, Solomon, wrote most of it. I think the reason God inspired Solomon to write these wise sayings in Proverbs because of his prayer and God's answer to him found in 1 Kings 3:9-14.

Why do you think that the Lord was pleased with this request from Solomon?

It is important for us to know the difference between knowledge and wisdom. Knowledge is knowing things. Wisdom is knowing when to use it. We also need to understand that true wisdom comes from God, reading His word and listening to His word spoken. Read Proverbs 2:6-7.

In the NLT Bible, verse 7 reads: *"He grants a treasure of common sense to the honest..."* This *"treasure of common sense"* sounds like something I want to have, how about you?

The foundation of wisdom is God. His word is the source of all truth and is the standard of truth by which we can measure everything. It makes sense then to know what the Bible has to say about different topics.

In Proverbs 1:7, what does it say is the beginning of knowledge?_____

What does fear mean in this verse?_____

Wisdom is closely connected with a true and intimate relationship with God. You've already made several wise choices in seeking that relationship. We'll never reach our full potential in the area of wisdom, but if we are actively seeking knowledge from the word of God, we can be confident that He will guide us through every situation that comes into our lives. See Proverbs 3:5-6.

One of the benefits of wisdom is good judgment in everyday life. Here is a true story that could have resulted in a disaster, but didn't:

You may have heard the story of Ivory soap, the "soap that floats". However, it was not always that way. Years ago, this soap was just another brand among many until a factory foreman made a mistake. He left a fresh batch of soap in the cooking vat and went to lunch. When he was late getting back and the soap had overcooked, the foreman frantically examined the burned soap.

It seemed to clean the same. The only difference he could see was in the weight. The burned soap was just lighter. He could either report the mistake and risk being fired, or he could make the best of it and ship the soap out as if nothing had happened. He shipped it out. The results surprised everyone. Instead of complaints, the company was deluged with orders for this new "floating soap" and the foreman was promoted.

Wisdom gives us the confidence to go with our instincts instead of feeling fearful and inadequate. Where would have that foreman have been if he didn't have the good judgment to see the possibilities in the "new floating soap"?

Look at Proverbs 3:21-22. If good judgment and discernment are like jewels or ornaments around our neck, what would bad judgment be compared to?

An important area in our lives where we could use a large amount of commonsense is in our relationships. Our relationship with God, first and foremost, and then our relationship with those we live with and are closest to. Next would probably be our extended family and church family and friends. And don't forget our neighbors, co-workers and even the people we see when we are shopping and at the doctor's offices. In other words, everyone on planet Earth. No matter how good our people skills are, we all could use the help from Proverbs.

Proverbs 3:7-8: *"Do not be wise in your own eyes; fear the Lord and shun evil. This will bring health to your body and nourishment to your bones."* NIV

How would you paraphrase this scripture to fit into today's language?

_____

_____

Here's another proverb on the wisdom of obedience to the Lord:

Proverbs 10:27—*"The fear of the LORD prolongs days, but the years of the wicked will be shortened."* NKJV

Remember that the word fear in this verse means reverent awe not being afraid. Put into your own words what reverent awe means.

Here are a few more gems on relationships from the Bible:

Proverbs 14:7
Proverbs 14:20
Proverbs 14:29
Proverbs 14:31
Proverbs 14:33

God is so good to give us the Proverbs where we can find simple, commonsense, sometimes humorous advice to help us in our everyday living here on planet Earth. Isn't it encouraging to you to know that God cares about not only the big things in our lives, but the little things as well?

He wants eternity for each of us personally. He wants also to give us the resources to live well during our time here on planet Earth in order to encourage as many as will take the journey with us. The book of Proverbs is one of the resources He provides to help us along.

Blessings!

# 50

# CHRISTMAS SELAH

Right about now, we are probably in panic mode wondering how (or even if) everything we want to do before Christmas will be accomplished. As hard as we try and as much as we want to have a quiet, simple, blessed Christmas holiday, stuff gets added to our to-do list and stress accompanies it.

The main problem as I see it sisters, is the fact that we are women and everything falls on us to make Christmas perfect in true "Martha" fashion. I'm talking about the Martha from the Bible and the other "today" Martha who guides us into all things necessary to make our holiday elegantly charming and unforgettable. (You all know who I'm talking about)

It's not our families who put this unwelcomed stress on us; it's our own feelings of inadequate perfection that drives us into the Christmas frenzy abyss and so let's not go down that road! Here is a good time to Selah (pause and ponder) the true focus of Christmas.

Because of God's Indescribable Gift (2 Corinthians 9:15) on the first Christmas, we are privileged to have received His gift of salvation and eternal life. Let the grace and mercy we've experienced at His hands fill our hearts and then flow through us to others. Allow ourselves to experience the wonder and joy of gratitude in this holy season.

## BARBARA GEER

I will be the first to confess that I like to decorate my house for Christmas. I enjoy the feeling it gives me and it is joyful to my spirit. I used to send cards to everyone I know, but I discovered that I don't like the pressure of having to do it, so I don't. I may send a few cards if I have time, but really, I would rather spend the time being with my family or making cookies. I try hard not to give in to the busyness of the season because that's a joy robber for me. You might like the busyness. It's really OK if we are different. Joy comes in many forms.

I think it's freeing to know the things that give your spirit a lift. You take the pressure off yourself when you give yourself permission to do the things that are meaningful to you. Family Christmas traditions are a way of drawing the family to each other and to God. What are some of the things you and your family do at Christmas time?

What are some things you would just as soon skip?

Above all let's not miss the inner sense of wonder that leads us to worship the One that gives the meaning to Christmas. It is the main thing, like the illustration in this little story:

"During the Great Depression that hit the United States in the 1930's, a family in the Midwest struggled to put food on their table. They had no money for luxuries.

One day posters all over town announced that a circus was coming. Admission would be $1. A boy in the family wanted to see the show, but his father told him that he would have to earn the money on his own. The youngster had never seen a circus before, so he worked feverishly and was able to buy a ticket.

On the day the circus arrived, he went to see the performers and the animals parade through town. As he watched, a clown came dancing over to him, and the boy put his ticket in the clown's hand. Then he stood on the curb and cheered as the rest of the parade moved by.

The boy rushed home to tell his parents what he had seen and how exciting the circus was. His father listened, then took his son in his arms and said, "Son, you didn't see the circus. All you saw was the parade."(author unknown)

Does this story grab your heart as it does mine? Have you ever lived out this little parable during a Christmas season? I'm sure most of us have. While buying and wrapping gifts, hiding presents from the children, or delivering them to neighbors, planning and attending parties, house cleaning and decorating, baking, choir or play practice and all the other wonderful holiday preparations that make up a portion of the Christmas season, what about the most important thing . . . the preparation of our hearts?

Look at Proverbs 4:23.

We consider the heart to be the core of our inner being. It's up to us to protect it according to this scripture. We can easily fail to guard it as we should during busy times. The enemy who is always on the prowl will certainly try his best to distract us when our guard is down. I've heard people say, "I can hardly wait until Christmas is over!" In fact, I've probably said it myself. When the preparation of our hearts is the focus of the Christmas season, we would be yearning for the time to linger not wanting it to be over.

During the season that we celebrate God's Indescribable Gift to us, it would be to our shame if we didn't take the time to worship Him with an attitude of joyful gratitude. Make a determination to make time to be still before Him with listening ears and quiet, expectant hearts. When we desire to feel His presence, He will reveal Himself to us. Scripture says when you seek Him with all your heart, you will find Him. (see Deuteronomy 4:29) This is a practice we would be blessed to continue all year long.

If only we would take time this Christmas season to listen, *really* listen to the voice of God as we are singing those familiar Christmas hymns. Or really see in our mind's eye the miracles of heaven—the virgin birth, the willingness of the maiden girl who carried the Savior of the world in her womb, the understanding and support of Joseph and so much more.

As we are busy with shopping, decorating and social events, let's set our hearts to worship and be thankful for this blessed event so many years ago. Let's think about the angels, the shepherds, the wise men who traveled so far to have a part. How did this blessed event change their lives? The angels were following God's orders, of course, but surely the sight of the "Babe" stirred them to worship Him with song.

The shepherds and the wise men must have been honored to be included. How do you think their lives were changed? Jesus came to change our lives as well. If we are too busy to see the "Main Thing" then we've missed the whole meaning of Christmas once again. Let's not let such a sacred opportunity go by. Let's us fix our eyes and hearts on the One who came for us. Let us be determined to set apart our hearts and minds to worship. Maybe others will see in us the Main event not the parade.

Make the most of this Christmas season. Do all the things that make you joyful and grateful to the One who left heaven so that we could have a right relationship with our Creator. Be involved only in activities that draw you and others closer to Jesus. Do all you can to make this a meaningful Christmas for your loved ones in the true sense of Christmas. Take time to pause and ponder God's love for you. Insist on daily quiet time to be alone with God.

Here are some scripture for you to reflect on during those times.

Isaiah 9:6—*"For unto us a Child is born, unto us a Son is given; and the government will be upon His shoulder. And His name will be called Wonderful, Counselor, Mighty God, Everlasting Father, Prince of Peace."* NKJV

Matthew 1:23—*"Behold, the virgin shall be with child, and bear a Son, and they shall call His name Immanuel," which is translated, "God with us."* NKJV

John 3:16-17—*"For God so loved the world that He gave His only begotten Son, that whoever believes in Him should not perish but have everlasting life. <sup>17</sup> For God did not send His Son into the world to condemn the world, but that the world through Him might be saved."* NKJV

John 3:36—*"He who believes in the Son has everlasting life; and he who does not believe the Son shall not see life, but the wrath of God abides on him."* NKJV

Here are some other verses to look up and reflect on God's goodness:

Luke 1:38—

Luke 2:10—

Luke 2:14—

2 Corinthians 9:15—

May
The warm,
Guiding star
Drive from your
Life every shadow;
May the glad song of
Angels find an echo in
Your heart; may the spirit
Of worship in the hearts of
The wise men, and the simple
Faith of the shepherds be yours
As, once more, you celebrate the
Birth-
Day of
A King.

Blessings!

# 51

# "GLORY TO GOD IN THE HIGHEST . . ."

Imagine you are a shepherd 2000 years ago working the night shift in the countryside near the small town of Bethlehem. Imagine your surprise when suddenly the sky lights up and an angel of the Lord descends from heaven and begins speaking to you and your shepherd friends. (You've never really seen an angel before, but who else could he be? This is too real to be a dream!) He tells you not to be afraid. (He must see you shaking under your tunic.) As he begins to talk, calm settles over you and you really begin to listen to the good news he was sent to tell you. He says it is good news, but it's pretty confusing, something about a baby in a manger—that's where animals are feed!

Again, suddenly the heavens open and a whole army (host) of angels appear praising God and saying . . . *"GLORY TO GOD IN THE HIGHEST, AND ON EARTH PEACE TO MEN ON WHOM HIS FAVOR RESTS."*

This magnificent sight must have been breath-taking! How kind of our Creator to arrange this event for a lowly audience of common folks as these shepherds. How many times do you think they repeated the details of all that happened that glorious night to their family, friends and probably anyone who would listen? These guys probably passed from this world to the next with this story on their lips. They were among the privileged few who saw their Savior as a Babe in a manger.

Let's take a closer look at this angelic declaration: *"Glory to God in the highest (heaven), and on earth peace among men with whom He is well pleased (men of goodwill, of His favor.)"* (Luke 2:14 AMP)

There are two elements in this verse that I want us to look at today. First is *"glory to God,"* and the second is *"and on earth peace among men"*. When we take the name of "Christ-follower" we have a privilege and a responsibility that goes with it. The privileges are many and the responsibilities are great and both belong in the "good thing" category. The means we have of knowing these blessings from God is through His Holy Word. I once read that there are over 30,000 promises in God's word. As we look at the following verses, discuss the key thought and whether it is a privilege or a responsibility.

Ephesians 4:29—What is the key thought?
Is it a privilege or a responsibility?

Psalm 19:14—What is the key thought?
Is it a privilege or a responsibility?

Psalm 46:1—What is the key thought?
Is it a privilege or a responsibility?

1 Peter 3:15—What is the key thought?
Is it a privilege or a responsibility?

1 Thessalonians 5:18—What is the key thought?
Is it a privilege or a responsibility?

Ephesians 2:8-9—What is the key thought?
Is it a privilege or a responsibility?

*"Glory to God in the highest"* is to live a life worthy of His name here on planet Earth. It is a life that includes willing obedience to His precepts, a genuine love for His people and a thankful heart. In Romans 12:1 the Word says we are *"to present our bodies as a living and holy sacrifice, acceptable to God, which is our spiritual service of worship."* (NASB) This sacrifice we are talking about is our love and devotion in response to the One who gives us unfailing love.

Look at Psalm 13:5 and Psalm 33:5 and Psalm 33:18 to read more about God's unfailing love.

Scripture states many times that His love surrounds us and . . ." *that neither death nor life, nor angels nor principalities nor powers, nor things present nor things to come, [39] nor height nor depth, nor any other created thing, shall be able to separate us from the love of God which is in Christ Jesus our Lord."* (Romans 8:38-39 NKJV) When we know of His love and have experienced it first hand, how can we keep from giving Him the glory due Him? *"Let everything that has breath praise the Lord." (*Psalm 150:6 NKJV)

The second element of our theme scripture says, *"And on earth peace among men."* In the history of our world there has been very few times of peace. This is true because after God gave man dominion over the earth, Adam and Eve sinned and the authority or power was transferred to Satan. We know some of Satan's other names—Prince of Darkness and Father of lies, etc. so the notion of peace is pretty hopeless. Right?

Peace in the New Testament is related the Old Testament concept of "shalom", meaning "wholeness, well-being and harmony with God and others." Notice in our theme scripture it says *"peace among men—**with whom He is well pleased, men of goodwill, of His favor**."* There is hope for those of us who love God and have said "yes" to His Son, Jesus, who is "the Prince of Peace."

Peace is not so much an external atmosphere as it is an inward experience. Peace is not the calm before the storm; it is the calm during the storm. As the Prince of Peace, Jesus offers His peace that pertains to three main relationships.

**First**, He enables us to have peace with God by His work of reconciliation. (His death and resurrection) Sin separated us from God, Jesus reconciled us with God. Because of Calvary, we are able to have a close relationship with our Creator. That intimacy brings peace and well-being to our souls.

**Second**, Jesus enables us to have peace within ourselves. He resolves the inner conflicts, cross purposes, and tensions which rob us of our peace. Through the work of the Holy Spirit within us, He can stop the war between our self-centered thoughts and our desire to do His will.

**And third**, when we are at peace with God and with ourselves, then we can be at peace with others. When the vertical relationship is right, then the horizontal relationship will take on its proper perspective.

Now, as good and easy as this all sounds, we know to achieve peace, there is lots of work involved. Peace in our lives is a process of developing it in our inner being. When the Holy Spirit took up residence within us, He brought peace along with other fruit of the Spirit. (Galatians 5:22-23) It is developed as our awareness of God's trustworthiness grows. Peace is produced in us as we trust Him little by little with our needs and concerns. It won't happen all at once. As you already know, we are a work in progress. (see Philippians 1:6)

It is good to know that peace is already inside us because of the Holy Spirit living in us, but how can we live out this virtue in practical ways when things seem to be falling apart or we feel stressed because of busyness?

One way I have found to have peace is to try and always have a positive attitude about people and not speculate about other people's actions. A wise person once said, "We should have much more peace if we would not busy ourselves with the sayings and doings of others." Try to accept people with all their faults, knowing that we all have a few odd tendencies ourselves. In Romans we are told *"if it is possible, as much as it depends on you, live peaceably with all men."* (12:18 NKJV)

Another way to experience peace in your heart is to not worry about not having enough to provide for you and your family. Sometimes thinking about the future can be overwhelming. You don't know what is going to happen anyway. Trust in the One who does. If God loved you enough to give His Son for you, you can believe He loves you enough to meet your needs. See Philippians 4:19 for the promise of God's provision.

> **"One of the best things about the future is that it comes one day at a time!"**

One way to **never** achieve peace in your heart is to be a people-pleaser for two reasons: one—it can't be done. There is no way you can please everyone all the time. And number two—your thoughts and actions are temporal. Be a God-pleaser and your thoughts and actions have eternal value.

If you don't feel peace in your heart today, make a determination to diligently pray for it and search God's Word for everything you can find on peace. This is a virtue that God wants us to experience in our daily lives. We are meant to have peace, it is our spiritual birthright. It is offered freely and has been paid for in full. Peace is ours for the asking and it is to our benefit to accept it from the hands of our Savior and then share it with others.

Colossians 3:15. *"And let the peace of God rule in your hearts, to which also you were called in one body; and be thankful."* (NKJV)

Blessings!

# 52

# ANGELS

**Those who take the Bible at full value cannot discount the subject of angels... The Scriptures mention their existence almost three hundred times.**—Billy Graham, from his book ANGELS

What is your experience with angels? Do you ever think about the spirit world—angels and demons, good and evil? Ever read a book or seen a movie or television program featuring angels? We are fascinated by stories of invisible, super-natural beings who are involved in a celestial good versus evil struggle.

Name some popular movies or books on the subject of angels.

A warning:
We must be careful as we study the subject of angels to not give them more credit or esteem than they deserve. They are created beings and not in any way on the same level as God. There are those who worship angels. Some say that angels are their personal channels to connect them with the spirits of friends and family who have passed on. They are greatly influenced by angels in their daily thoughts and actions. There are even classes in our schools and colleges that teach about angels and their supposed ability to advise us.

This is wrong thinking. We as Christian women need to know what we believe. And for that information, we must go to the source of truth—the Bible. God's Word makes it clear that the subject of angels calls for a good deal of discernment and caution. The unseen world can either be harmful or helpful. Therefore, it must be taken more seriously than a passing curiosity.

Angels are not men who've died and become angels who help people here on planet earth. They are _____. Look at Psalm 91:11 and Psalm 103:20.

"Highway to Heaven" was great entertainment but not true to God's Word. God created spiritual beings called angels for the purpose of_____. See Hebrews 1:14.

God has created angels, in part, to minister to us and according to Hebrews 12:22 there are _____ of them.

Angels are not to be _____. See Revelation 19:10 and Exodus 20:3

Angels do not have the ability to be every where at once. Only God _____. Acts 17:24-27

Only God is omnipresent. That's one of God's non-transferrable attributes... meaning that only God can possess that quality. Some of God's other non-transferrable attributes are:

SOVEREIGN . . . Number one, supreme

ETERNAL . . . always was, is, and shall be

OMNISCIENT . . . God possesses all knowledge. Angels have more knowledge than us, but it comes from God.

OMIPOTENT . . . All powerful. Angels are stronger than us humans. Daniel 6:22 tells us that it only took one angel to shut the lion's mouth!

IMMUTABLE . . . That means God never changes. Hebrews 13:8 says that: *"Jesus Christ, the same yesterday, today, and tomorrow."*

All this is to say that we must keep things in proper prospective. God is God and His reign is forever. While angels are created beings who worship and serve Him and are sent out by Him to minister to the "heirs of salvation." (US)

# AM I MY SISTER'S KEEPER?

Most of us have never seen an angel or at least we didn't recognize them as such, because although they sometimes do appear in human form, it's rare.

The following true story is taken from Dr. Graham's book:

Dr. S.W. Mitchell, a celebrated Philadelphia neurologist, had gone to bed after an exceptionally tiring day. Suddenly he was awakened by someone knocking on his door. Opening it he found a little girl poorly dressed and deeply upset. She told him her mother was very sick and asked him if he would please come with her. It was a bitterly cold, snowy night, but though he was bone tired, Dr. Mitchell dressed and followed the girl.

As Reader's Digest reports the story, he found the mother desperately ill with pneumonia. After arranging for medical care, he complimented the sick woman on the intelligence and persistence of her little daughter. The woman looked at him strangely and then said, "My daughter died a month ago." She added, "Her shoes and coat are in the clothes closet there." Dr. Mitchell, amazed and perplexed, went to the closet and opened the door. There hung the very coat worn by the little girl who had brought him to tend to her mother. It was warm and dry and could not possibly have been out in the wintry night.

Could the doctor have been called in the hour of desperate need by an angel who appeared as this woman's young daughter? Was this the work of God's angels on behalf of the sick woman?

Of course, we don't know the answer to that. Only God knows. We do know however, that He can work out His divine plan by any means He cares to. What should be remarkable to us and beyond our comprehension is the fact that God loves us and is at work in human affairs. Mine, yours, and everyone's on planet Earth. When we hear these unexplainable stories, we must assume that God is in control and everything will turn out for the best. Praise God!

Let's look to the Word for other facts about angels.

According to Psalm 103:20, what do angels do?

What emotion do angels experience in Luke 15:10 and what is the reason for it?

One important fact that we do know about angels is that one of their duties is to help people. Do you believe you have a guardian angel? Many of us have grown up believing it to be so. Not only is it comforting to think that some superhuman being is looking out for us, but some of us have even experienced an amazing circumstance where the results simply defy physical laws.

Matthew 18:10-11 suggest that each one of us has our own personal guardian angel. Read and discuss your opinion.

Two other verses talk about angels being around us and protecting us. Look at Psalm 34:7 and Psalm 91:9-14.

Even if we don't have a specific angel assigned to us, what assurances do these 4 verses give us?

Look at the eye-opening account 2 Kings 6:15-17:

*"And when the servant of the man of God arose early and went out, there was an army, surrounding the city with horses and chariots. And his servant said to him, "Alas, my master! What shall we do?"*

*So he answered, "Do not fear, for those who are with us are more than those who are with them." And Elisha prayed, and said, "LORD, I pray, open his eyes that he may see." Then the LORD opened the eyes of the young man, and he saw. And behold, the mountain was full of horses and chariots of fire all around Elisha."* (NKJV)

Does it encourage or frighten you (or both) to consider the possibility that beings from the spirit realm are around even when we can't see, hear or sense their presence? Explain

Angelic appearances happened often in the life of Jesus and we know the accounts so well that we might not appreciate them as we should. Jesus' life was certainly supernatural from beginning to end. His important mission here on planet Earth, called for special support from heaven.

An angel named _____ first appeared to Mary in Luke 1:26-33.

What was the good news that the angel came to share with Mary?

# AM I MY SISTER'S KEEPER?

An angel of the Lord also appeared to Mary's uncle, Zechariah several months prior to his visit with Mary. What was Gabriel's good news to him? See Luke 1:11-17.

An angel of the Lord appeared to Joseph as well. Read the account in Matthew 1:18-21. This time the mission was one of assurance. How good God is to be so concerned about our feelings and doubts.

The angels again appeared . . . this time to announce to the shepherds the birth of the Savior. Read that account in Luke 2:8-20.

Interesting isn't it, that the angels announced Jesus' birth to the shepherds, but the wise men had to follow a star? I wonder why. What do you think?

Why do you think that the first thing the angels usually say is, "Do not be afraid!"?

What might be your response if an angel of the Lord appeared to you?

What would the story of Jesus' earthly birth be like to you without the angel's involvement?

Most of the angelic appearances to the individuals concerning Jesus' here on earth were from the angel Gabriel. There are two other named angels in the Bible. They are _____ who is called an archangel, in charge of other angels. You can read about him in Jude 9, Daniel 10:21 and other places. The other named angel is _____. He is also called Satan, the Devil or the evil one. He is the fallen angel because he was kicked out of heaven for thinking he could take over God's position. (There are no openings for that position.)

Angels have been written about in special studies and portrayed in various ways in books, art and movies. For centuries people have even prayed to angels. A definite no-no. (Refer to #1 commandment in Exodus 20.) We must keep our view of angels in balance according to God's Word. One of our most important tasks is to understand the ultimate purpose of angels in our lives and to see them in the context of God's glory.

Blessings!

# STEPS TO A NEW LIFE PLAN OF SALVATION

You can be free from the guilt of your past and have an assuring hope for the future. The good news is that God loves you and has a wonderful plan for your life.

John 3:16 NKJV

*"For God so loved the world that He gave His only begotten Son, that whoever believes in Him should not perish but have everlasting life."*

STEP ONE—Acknowledge your past—Roman 3:23 NKJV

*"For all have sinned and fall short of the glory of God."*

Man was created to have fellowship with God, but because of his own stubborn self-will, he chose to go his own independent way and fellowship with God was broken. This attitude of rebellion or indifference, is what the Bible calls sin.

STEP TWO—Invite Christ into your life—John 1:12 NKJV

*"But as many as received Him, to them He gave the right to become children of God, to those who believe in His name"*

Revelation 3:20 NKJV

*"Behold, I stand at the door and knock. If anyone hears My voice and opens the door, I will come in to him and dine with him, and he with Me."*

Receiving Christ involves turning to God from self, trusting Christ to come into our lives, to forgive our sins and to make us what He wants us to be. You can receive Christ right now through prayer. (Just asking Him)

**"Lord Jesus,**

**I admit that I have sinned against You. I am sorry for my sin and I trust You to forgive me. Come into my life and help me to serve You. Make me the kind of person You want me to be. Amen"**

STEP THREE—Trust God's forgiveness—1 John 1:9 NKJV

*"If we confess our sins, He is faithful and just to forgive us of our sins and to cleanse us from all unrighteousness."*

We must confess our sins to Jesus to receive forgiveness. And we must admit that we are to blame for our sins. Jesus Christ is God's only provision for man's sin. Through Him you can know and experience God's love and plan for your life.

STEP FOUR—Declare your faith in Christ—Matthew 10:32 NKJV

*"Therefore whoever confesses Me before men, him I will also confess before My Father who is in heaven.*

Don't keep this wonderful news a secret. Tell someone right away. That action will begin to cement your commitment to God. It is the beginning of a life-long journey here on this earth and into eternity!

The moment that you, as an act of faith, received Christ, many things happened, including the following:

1. Christ came into your life. (Revelation 3:20 and Colossians 1:27)
2. Your sins were forgiven. (Colossians 1:14)
3. You became a child of God. (John 1:12)
4. You began the great adventure for which God created you. (John 10:10, 2 Corinthians 5:17 and 1 Thessalonians 5:18)

# Answers to God 101 work sheet

1. Holy
2. Kind
3. Rock
4. Mighty
5. Majestic
6. Gracious
7. Powerful
8. Redeemer
9. Forgiving
10. Deliverer
11. Wonderful
12. Righteous
13. Trustworthy
14. Compassionate
15. Understanding

# ABOUT THE AUTHOR

Barbara's greatest passion is encouraging and teaching women to study the Word. She believes that the Bible is the standard of truth. Truth and knowledge give us more confidence and freedom as God's women.

Over the years she has lead many Bible studies and discipled new Christians one-on-one. Currently, she is leading a weekly Bible study called PEARLS which stands for **P**raying, **E**ncouraging, **A**ffirming, **R**eaching, **L**oving, and **S**erving. Barbara believes those are some of the qualities that we as God's women should strive to have.

Contact her at Facebook or visit her blog at www.barbgeer.blogspot.com

Made in the USA
Middletown, DE
19 May 2019